AMERICAN NEUTRALITY IN THE 20TH CENTURY:
The Impossible Dream

JOHN N. PETRIE

McNair Paper 33
January 1995

INSTITUTE FOR NATIONAL STRATEGIC STUDIES

NATIONAL DEFENSE UNIVERSITY
Washington, DC

INSS publishes McNair Papers to provoke thought and inform discussion on issues of U.S. national security in the post–Cold War era. These monographs present current topics related to national security strategy and policy, defense resource management, international affairs, civil-military relations, military technology, and joint, combined, and coalition operations.

Opinions, conclusions, and recommendations, expressed or implied, are those of the authors. They do not necessarily reflect the views of the National Defense University, the Department of Defense, or any other U.S. Government agency. Cleared for public release; distribution unlimited.

For those in peril on the sea . . .
those who have been . . .
and those, like my father,
who rest in peace beneath it.
May their experience shorten the list of
sailors who might join them in the future.

Contents

ACKNOWLEDGMENTS

This work would not have been possible without the assistance, guidance, patience, and understanding of many fine people. It would be impossible to pay appropriate attention to the contributions of each in this brief statement. The contributions of a few, however, cannot go unmentioned.

Professor Alfred P. Rubin of the Fletcher School of Law and Diplomacy, whom I met when he held the Stockton Chair of International Law at the Naval War College, through his support, guidance, and encouragement, more than anyone else, has made completion of this effort possible. The quality of this work is in large part the result of Professor Rubin's advice and counsel. Its deficiencies are my own.

Together with his colleagues the late Professor Leo Gross of the Fletcher School and Howard S. Levie, Professor Emeritus of the St. Louis University School of Law and Adjunct Professor (for life) at the Naval War College, Professor Rubin provided me with an understanding of not only the meaning of the law but more importantly its inescapable influence upon international relations in general. It was with Professor Levie that I began this work. I wrote its first draft as a paper for his law of war course at Naval War College. Since then, the Howard S. Levie Chair of Military Operational Law has been named in his honor. I received, more than instruction, inspiration from this gifted and insightful trio of gentlemen lawyers who nurtured the interest in the law which resulted in the present work. These men provided me with a perspective on the international scene and the effect of international law on my profession which prepared me for my duties in a manner few are afforded.

Mr. Frank Uhlig, Jr., long time Editor, now Editor Emeritus, of the Naval War College Press provided opportunities and encouragement for—and recommendations to improve—my writing since we first met in the early 80's. His personal help with the manuscript was indispensible.

The greatest gifts these four men bestowed upon me are their patience with my shortcomings and their friendship despite them.

Ms. Melissa Stack, my research assistant at National War College when the final draft was prepared also deserves special mention. Her hours in the library made it possible to finish this, carry a full teaching load, and fulfill my responsibilities in the Dean's Office.

Finally, my wife Ann and our three children, Alex, Noel, and Sean, gave me the support, patience, and understanding which made the long hours away from them—even though working in the same house—possible. Ann frequently assumed the thankless roles of proofreader and style editor. Each of the children took their turn in the essential but lackluster task of "gofer". Later, Alex personally made the completion of this work possible. He put his college education in "Information Systems" to work to help me defeat my most formidable adversary in this effort—my computer.

Most importantly though, the family sacrificed opportunities that will never come again to give me the chance to fulfill this goal. I can never adequately repay this gift of love.

PREFACE

This work began with a paper written in the spring of 1982 as a student at the College of Command and Staff at the Naval War College. My professional and personal interest in the Laws of War and Neutrality were nurtured throughout those studies and grew during master's and doctoral work at the Fletcher School of Law and Diplomacy. Each international crisis since has confirmed my belief that a more thorough consideration of this body of law could better inform policy makers.

The chronology that follows demonstrates that the United States found the requirements of strict neutrality less than useful for fulfilling its policy imperatives throughout the 20th century. The reasons for this are varied, but all involve departures from the strict impartiality required of neutrals. The common thread running through them is that global interests make impartiality difficult to maintain and often counterproductive. It also becomes clear that this will continue for the future.

Although the incidents explored stretch back over 100 years, history is not its focus. Incidents are cited only to show their relationship to the pattern of U.S. behavior; historical details are not elaborated. Further, incidents are looked at in the context of what was known at the time, without the benefit of hindsight. The loss of the battleship *MAINE*, for example, is now believed to have resulted from an accident; at the time it was believed to have been an attack.

The detailed behavior of other nations was also not examined except in response to that of the United States, because while this work is about international law, it is for the U.S. naval force and unit commanders who must understand that law. My personal knowledge of and involvement in highly sensitive U.S. policy implementation in Central America and Panama in the mid-1980s requires that those examples not be treated. This exclusion does not detract from the product and removes even the question of whether classified material was used in any way in the preparation of this work.

Our grandfathers had to make decisions with much less information and, like today, the initial reports were sometimes flawed. In some ways, therefore, the imperfections obvious in the contemporary accounts recorded in newspapers provide a better context than the more thorough and better informed historical accounts. In other places, historians' work is used extensively to document the details of incidents. This is especially true for the period immediately preceding World War II because so many significant examples occured then.

With a focus on identifying a pattern of departures from the strict impartiality of neutrality, the account that follows resists, as much as possible, the temptation to explore other fascinating aspects of the incidents dealt with.

AMERICAN NEUTRALITY IN THE 20TH CENTURY:
The Impossible Dream

1.
INTRODUCTION

*International relations is neither a science nor a pure
subject. Its purpose, its utility, and its justification
depend on the ability of scholars to offer theoretical
concepts which will assist practitioners in identifying
the choices that confront them.*[1]

Better understanding of the requirements of neutrality and the
dangers of unneutral U.S. policy can improve responsiveness and
mission effectiveness in some critical situations and provide
information to decisionmakers to facilitate the safe and effective
employment of naval forces as an instrument of U.S. policy. To
this end arose the desire to explore issues of international law
affecting operations of the U.S. Navy at sea, which in turn
resulted in this book.

Naval forces are recruited and trained, and their ships and
equipment are procured and maintained, to implement and
support the policy decisions of the United States. The intent here

---

[1]James Cable, *Diplomacy at Sea* (Annapolis: Naval Institute Press, 1985),
34.

is to provide a better understanding of the legal environment that surrounds and is affected by these policy decisions, in order to improve the ability to assess future situations and their attendant costs and risks—thus enhancing the safety and effectiveness of our valuable and limited naval assets. To do this it is necessary to review the legal issues involved in past situations to broaden the understanding of those involved with naval forces. This improved perspective should assist these participants to make better informed and more effective naval policy decisions and in turn, provide clearer guidance for the at-sea commander.

If this work facilitates the performance of naval forces in their conduct of peacetime missions or their preparation for combat, or if only a list of important generic questions is developed by decisionmakers, there is value to this effort. And if the operating forces are made safer because of this study, there could be no higher reward.

The analyses focus upon the relationship of the law of neutrality to the actions of the United States in a series of situations that stretch back to the 1890s. Its purpose is to show that the interests of the United States repeatedly have required the use of naval forces as a tool of U.S. policy in areas where combat was already underway or the opening of hostilities was imminent.

The behavior of the United States frequently did not comply with the impartiality that, despite the major changes in the international system over the past 100 years, remains an obligation of neutrality. Often, the partiality of the United States drew U.S. forces into the conflict or contributed to that end by precipitating mutual self-defense situations or actions in defense of conflicting rights.[2]

---

[2]States frequently justify their actions as self-defense of rights or anticipatory self-defense. When this happens in response to the threat of force by a second party, that second party can in turn claim self-defense against the use of force. Conflicting rights such as those involved in disputed territory or disputed rights to use ocean space are another case where the law not only admits the opportunity to defend rights but may seem to require confrontation— although diplomatic protests are always appropriate. Claims to rights contested by another state may require exercise of the asserted rights to avoid counter- claims of acquiescence. The claimed rights can only be unequivocally upheld

Decisions taken in support of U.S. interests and policy objectives produced this pattern of behavior—but the risks attendent to it have increased. Now more than ever before, U.S. naval policy must be shaped to also consider other states' assessments of the legal situation. This is an important factor today in risk analysis, mission planning, and guidance to naval force commanders.

The historical review of U.S. practice regarding the law of neutrality is not supposed to be a comprehensive treatment of all U.S. actions but is intended solely to present an extensive, protracted, and consistent body of evidence to support the legal and policy analysis herein.

Naval planners must examine the legal environment in which our ships might operate, and this study continues what the Navy has always done to improve future operations:

• Understand the operating environment and seek to exploit its benefits and minimize its hazards

• Review operations and identify "lessons learned"

• Examine innovations, discover their applicability to the profession, and develop their optimal use.

Implementing a policy partial to one side in a conflict signals a change in the legal environment, much as a sudden drop in barometric pressure indicates a change in weather. Understanding this aspect of the law can be an important factor for making decisions regarding naval forces. It can also provide an essential warning to them, because when partiality is appropriate to U.S. policy objectives, naval forces in proximity to another nation's war can be at risk. Further, a review of U.S. policy and practice in previous international situations in which the Navy played a role provides a clarity today that decisionmakers of the past did not enjoy. The "lessons learned" include the importance of considering the belligerent's view of U.S. actions under the law of neutrality, a perspective that illuminates the risks involved.

---

through by exercising them. They can most effectively be denied by the contending party defending their legal interpretation of the "rights" involved. Requirements to assert and deny rights by contending parties are a formula for confrontation which unfortunately is embedded in the law.

The consistent pattern of U.S. behavior shows that impartial conduct, the essence of neutrality, was either not possible or not the preferred option of the United States. This pattern of partiality now typifies U.S. practice, and it will likely continue. If this is true, innovations in operations, the law, and their interface are appropriate.

ASSUMPTIONS AND CONSIDERATIONS

This work proceeds from two assumptions:

- A review of historical events better enables us to predict the behavior of states in similar circumstances. Even where prediction is not possible, forces are at play which continue to influence future events and must be considered.
- International law influences the formation and execution of foreign policy.

These assumptions do not mean the historian is tantamount to soothsayer[3] or that states blindly obey international law. An examination of history reveals a pattern of responses to similar problems or situations; the pattern is evidence of a set of subtle priorities prevailing over more transient influences on the interests of statesmen or states. It is likely these priorities will again influence decisionmaking when circumstances approximate any historical precedent.

Whether international law drives the decision or not, it is almost always a factor in the decisionmaking process. Even when the issue or legal concept being considered is not uniformly acknowledged as law by all states, but merely as the reasonable expectation of other affected states, the very recognition of this expectation is evidence of the influence exerted. Disregarding international law has inescapable consequences,[4] and while not

---

[3]On the other hand, much can be learned and predicted if we heed Sir James Cable's warning that, "There is always a temptation for historians commenting on contemporary events to emulate the legendary Chinaman, in the early years of this (20th) century, who considered it distinctly premature to describe the consequences of the French Revolution of 1789." Cable, 22.

[4]"International law has the character and qualities of law, and serves the functions and purposes of law, providing restraints against arbitrary state action and guidance in international relations. . . . States, the principal addressees of

always immediately perceptible, they are inevitable. The costs accruing to a state that ignores international law can span a broad spectrum, from a minimal loss of prestige or influence to use of force by affected states. It must be recognized that when the practice of states is, or is in the process of being, elevated to the status of law through consistent compliance or voluntary commitment, it also constitutes an expectation by the international community that cannot be ignored with impunity.[5] Even when state practice constitutes a new precedent that might eventually modify customary international law, existing law is the baseline from which new law evolves, and it will be consciously considered in deciding to take the action that establishes the precedent. When positive (treaty) law is at issue, its influence is even greater because a state's good faith, its word, is unquestionably involved.

States are the actors in the international system. They design and implement the law. They are also the seat of what is accepted as international authority, so the way the distribution of authority in the current international political system affects behavior must also be considered. This authority defines the

---

international law, treat it as law, consider themselves bound by it, attend to it with a sense of legal obligation and with concern for the consequences of a violation." American Law Institute, *Restatement of the Law (Third): The Foreign Relations Law of the United States (Rest. 3rd)* (St. Paul, MN: American Law Institute, 1987), 1:17. The Restatement 3rd is an unofficial analysis of U.S. interpretations of the law regarding foreign policy and determined by editors and commentators writing for the American Law Institute. While it is not the official U.S. Government position it is a reasonable assessment based upon practice and pronouncements. It is used herein to provide the benefits of both a professional analysis of U.S. practice and an assessment of the U.S. position where none might otherwise have been articulated or even developed for a specific situation or question.

[5]"In the international system, law is observed because of a combination of forces, including the unarticulated recognition by states generally of the need for order, and of their common interest in maintaining particular norms and standards, as well as every state's desire to avoid the consequences of violation. . . . That states (governments) make law, interpret law for their own guidance, and respond to interpretations and actions by others, makes for a complex legal-political-diplomatic process, but it is no less 'legal' even if it is less structured than domestic law in developed national societies." *Rest. 3rd*, 1:19.

boundaries of outside influence on the internal events and processes of states and their willingness to undertake obligations to others. In sum, this authority constitutes the essence of a state's autonomy—its ability to make unfettered internal and external decisions. Actions taken in disregard of this distribution of authority are likely to prove futile or provoke unwanted and unhelpful reactions.[6]

When involved in an armed conflict, this is the authority other states use to determine their rights and options to respond to perceived U.S. policy. They rely upon U.S. pronouncements, official and informal; pre-conceived notions of the U.S. agenda regarding their dispute and its resolution; and actions they interpret as intended to support and implement their view of U.S. policy. Further, the laws of war and neutrality proceed from the practice of states and represent a balance of rights and responsibilities. The logic underpinning these laws is sound, and actions defying that logic will bring responses. If it is not understood that the logic is being ignored, those responses may be unanticipated.

Using these assumptions as a point of departure, the nexus of the policy and legal processes mentioned above—and their pragmatic consequences when executing policy—are examined in this book.[7] Key questions addressed are:

---

[6]"The decisionmakers made authoritative by the perspectives of effective participants in the world arena include not only the various officials of nation-states but also the officials of international governmental organizations, as well as judges of international courts and of specifically constituted arbitral tribunals. . . . the very fact that the state official is on some occasions an authoritative decisionmaker for public world order and on other occasions a claimant requires of the official the promise of reciprocity in all his decisions and claims. From this necessary reciprocity arises the recognition and clarification of a community interest which permits an appropriate compromise of competing claims and affords sanction for decision." Myres S. McDougal and William T. Burke, *The Public Order of the Oceans: A Contemporary International Law of the Sea* (New Haven: New Haven Press, 1987), 36-37.

[7]"Law is the result of social life and evolves with it, it is, to a large extent, the effect of politics—especially of a collective kind—as practiced by the States. We must therefore beware of considering law and politics as mutually antagonistic. Each of them should be permeated by the other." International Court of Justice (ICJ), Report of Judgments, Advisory Opinions and Orders

- Can the United States reasonably expect to comply with strict neutrality in an interdependent world?
- Will other states accept unneutral—or so-called non-belligerent—behavior by the United States while the nation asserts a neutral policy?
- If not, what must the at-sea commander understand?
- How can the at-sea commander better be supported regarding these questions?

THE LAW OF NEUTRALITY AND RELATIVE COMBAT POWER

In this century the United States became both economically and strategically interdependent with most of the rest of the world. Consequently, most armed conflicts arising since the Spanish-American War involved at least the peripheral interests of either the United States or an ally. This consistently resulted in the United States being unable to remain impartial, or at least in a decision that purposely or accidentally abandoned impartiality. The United States frequently articulated a neutral policy, meaning it would abstain from direct participation in the hostilities as a belligerent, but repeatedly executed a policy that did not meet the baseline criterion (impartiality) of the law of neutrality.[8]

(1949), *Corfu Channel Case*—Individual Opinion of Judge Alvarez, 41-42.

[8]This requirement for impartiality is clear in the codifications which will be addressed later, but those treaties are generally decades old. A contemporary view of this aspect of the law, however, confirms this criterion has not yet changed even though state practice frequently fails to adhere to it strictly. Specifically, " The neutral state is obliged to be impartial, that is to say it may not engage in the war or support one or the other of the belligerent states." Count Wilhelm Wachtmeister, Ambassador of Sweden to the United States, "Neutrality and International Order", A Lecture Delivered at the United States Naval War College, Newport, RI, 21 March 1989. The quote is from a draft of the speech provided to the author. An adaptation of the speech was later published in *Naval War College Review* (*NWCR*) (Spring 1990), 105-114.

In an article entitled "The Concept of Neutrality in International Law" in the *Denver Journal of International Law* 16:2/3 (1988), 353-375, Professor Alfred P. Rubin, of the Fletcher School of Law and Diplomacy *inter alia* traces the development of U.S. Neutrality Laws and demonstrates that they have resulted more in response to domestic considerations than to assure U.S. compliance with international law requirements for neutrals. See especially 366

The rights and duties of neutrals and belligerents in time of armed conflict are not mere legalistic rhetoric—they represent a carefully balanced relationship in which neutrals do not interfere with the policy goals of belligerents in exchange for a broad immunity from the violence used to attain those goals by belligerents. Impartiality intends to prevent the actions of a neutral nation from giving unbalanced support to one belligerent at the expense of another. The law is the codification of sound policy decisions and the military principle of economy of force. Absent the law, the logical consequences would not be much different.

Partiality costs the United States some of the legal protections afforded a neutral nation. The initial impact of losing these protections frequently is negligible as belligerent parties choose not to exercise the full range of belligerent rights when such exercise would potentially convert an imperfect neutral to a confirmed and exceptionally powerful enemy. Put another way, the protection of law the United States surrendered from time to time through partiality was not immediately obvious, because it was replaced in practice by other protections. The preponderant military capability of the United States, and the perception by the aggrieved belligerent that U.S. national will would support its use, gave pause. The more an aggrieved belligerent has to lose, the longer and more carefully its leadership considers whether they should exercise the legal right of reprisal or otherwise react adversely to the unneutral U.S. action.

High-technology weaponry in the hands of potential adversaries now makes this seemingly inescapable partiality a greater risk for U.S. naval forces. The relationships requiring U.S. partiality and the availability of relatively inexpensive ship-killing (or at least mission-killing) weapons will increase throughout the foreseeable future. Concurrently, the protections substituted for the law in the past will become relatively more important and potentially less persuasive. Because the United States did not need to weigh these considerations as heavily in the past, there is reason to anticipate a period of adjustment, a period that will witness belligerent states (or other entities that

---

and 371.

may exercise belligerent rights) testing their increase in relative combat power against the willingness of the United States to respond in kind.[9]

DEFINITIONS AND CLARIFICATIONS

Before beginning the analysis, it is useful to explain the manner in which some terms are being used, in order to minimize ambiguity.

Naval Policy

"Naval policy" cannot be assigned a precise definition; although used in many applications conveying the same general sense, it will often have shades of meaning. Here, "naval policy" describes the collective decisions, and the actions which result from their execution, affecting the employment, support, mobility options, and even procurement and outfitting of naval forces in peacetime. These decisions and actions do not always originate in the Department of the Navy; some are the purview of the President, both when acting as Commander-in-Chief and in his domestic and international political roles. Related to the President's sphere are matters decided or announced by certain Members of Congress or officials of the Departments of State, Defense, or Justice.

The relationships of these decisions and actions to naval forces may be intuitively obvious or exceptionally subtle; in some cases, the Department of the Navy initially may not even be

---

[9]The term relative combat power is used in the broadest sense here. It not only considers the comparison of national orders of battle but the forces which are available at the scene of the action at the moment of decision as this determines the chances of tactical success for the specific operation. For example, "A navy operating at a distance not only needs more ships to deploy even an equal force, but special kinds of ships: ocean-going warships, aircraft carriers, a fleet train. The navy operating in its own waters, on the other hand, may be able to make effective use of much cheaper vessels—missile firing patrol craft or coastal submarines—whose lack of sea-keeping qualities is no impediment close off shore. They can be supported by land based aircraft, even by coastal artillery or missiles. Mining is also easier for the coastal state. Last, but emphatically not least, a state conducting a conflict in its own waters can commit all its forces.", Cable, 40.

aware of them. But, when the ability of the Navy to fulfill its missions in support of national policy in peace or national strategy in war is affected, or those missions are being fulfilled, naval policy is being made or executed.

Policy Process

The policy of the United States is developed within a democratic and constitutional framework. This frequently results in actions flowing more directly from the constitutional or bureaucratic processes among the branches of government than from decisionmaking by those charged with the development and execution of foreign policy. (Policy development and execution can even be affected by different positions taken by agencies within the executive branch).[10] When analyzing the history of the United States, therefore, a pattern of behavior may emerge that does not necessarily reflect policy decisions or national priorities but, more accurately, the policy execution resulting from domestic political and bureaucratic processes.

Policy execution is often observed by other states while U.S. intentions may be both unknown and inconsequential; therefore, the behavior of the United States can be examined without always understanding what was intended. In some cases, it will be clear that behavior directly contradicted intended policy, and it is this U.S. behavior, and its impact upon the affected states' own national interests, by which those affected states will judge U.S. compliance with international law and their policy options to exercise rights under it.

While intention and stated policy are certainly mitigating factors in any assessment, they will be given weight proportionate to the credibility the United States enjoys in the state evaluating the actions. Equally important, U.S. action in large part

---

[10]"The system of checks and balances, fundamental as it may be to the American democracy, markedly detracts, not only from unity of command (save in periods of dire national emergency), but even from the possibility of coherent and consistent policy formation". James Schlesinger, "The Office of the Secretary of Defense" in Robert J. Art, Vincent Davis, and Samuel P. Huntington, eds., *Reorganizing America's Defense: Leadership in War and Peace* (Washington: Pergammon-Brassey's, 1985), 255-274 at 256.

determines other states' reactions. Simply put, other states respond based upon their perceptions of what the United States *does* and *says*, not what the President of the United States *intends* to do or *means* by what he says.[11] Consequently, the term "U.S. policy" will be understood in this broad context.

Intent

Naval policy is affected by the legal, political, and tactical environment in which ships operate. This environment is defined by the actions naval forces must take to execute the policy of the United States; the expectations, perceptions, and reactions of states affected by that execution; our relative power relationship to the affected states; and the perception of each state's will to use its power to have a particular policy prevail. After examining the current status of the law of neutrality, the behavior of the United States with regard to that law and the events that may have influenced the law's development throughout this century will be reviewed in chronological order.

The behavior of the United States results from priorities and patterns of decisionmaking it was compelled to respond and conform to (or at least repeatedly has) since this country assumed the role of a global power, roughly a century ago. These priorities and processes, however subtle, can be expected to continue to affect the execution of policy. Therefore, the behavior in previous cases helps to understand forces that may influence the actions of the United States in similar future situations.

In future conflicts, the consequences of actions that establish the partiality of the United States will prove more challenging to the commanders of naval forces in an increasingly dangerous operating environment. The ability to identify and understand the

---

[11]"A state is responsible for any violation of its obligations under international law resulting from action or inaction by

(a) the government of the state,

(b) the government or authorities of any political subdivision of the state, or

(c) any organ, agency, official, employee, or other agent of a government or of any political subdivision, acting within the scope of authority or under color of such authority." *Rest. 3rd,* 207, 1:96.

point at which partiality might affect the legal—and consequently the tactical—situation will make at-sea commanders more sensitive and alert, reducing the risk of these challenging situations.

NEUTRALITY IN THE MODERN WORLD

Under international law, neutrality is simply the condition of a state or government which refrains from taking part, directly or indirectly, in a war between other powers. . . . It is in any case, unattainable for a great power in the modern world.[12]

Before a reasonable assessment of neutral obligations can be pursued, it is necessary to examine briefly the legal concept of neutrality and the effect the practice of states may be having on this concept.

The United States began to exercise the role of world power about the time of the Spanish-American War. Examination of potential changes to the law of neutrality and the behavior of the United States in light of the law will therefore focus on events since the interests of the United States forced consideration of intervention into the civil war in Cuba.

"When Cicero wrote, *inter arma silent legis*, he emphasized [the] generally accepted antithesis between law and violence."[13] If one wonders how a law can purport to regulate the brutal character of war, the answer is quite simple: it must. It must, for very practical reasons. The most basic reason was explained by Glaucon in Plato's "Republic":

When men have both done and suffered injustice and have had experience of both, not being able to avoid the one and obtain

---

[12]Manfred Jonas, *Isolationism in America* (New York: Cornell University Press, 1964). 203.

[13]Quincy Wright, *A Study of War,* Abridged Edition (Chicago: University of Chicago Press, 1964), 173. The internal quote is roughly translated, "In war the law is silent."

the other, they think that they had better agree among themselves to have neither; hence there arise laws and mutual covenants; and that which is ordained by law is termed by them lawful and just.[14]

The "laws" that have been codified to regulate war's intensity and prevent its spread to neutrals are not always logical to the objective analyst, but they reflect what was thought possible and practical in their historical context. They are also the result of compromises that probably varied from what some might consider an ideal, morally just position in proportion to the relative power relationship, the basic motivation, and the skill and persuasiveness of negotiators, as perceived by the contending parties. By 1907 the traditional roles of sovereign states in time of armed conflict were codified to the extent that the rights and responsibilities of states were clearly articulated and broadly accepted. But changes in both the power relationships and perceptions of relative advantage, from the time of codification to the time of actual engagement of forces, resulted in less than scrupulous adherence to all the negotiated rules.

Legally, war was two isolated entities clashing to impose their wills upon one another, no matter how briefly; third states were considered neutral and were to have no direct or indirect part in the war.[15] The law of war applied between belligerents and the law of neutrality applied between belligerents and neutrals.[16] While the theory was clear, practice often involved

---

[14]Plato, "The Republic", Book II, 358-359, in William Chase Greene, ed., *The Dialogues of Plato*, translated by Benjamin Jowett (New York: Liveright, 1927), 272. Plato later partially refutes this logic but he is arguing for an ideal state of being. The "law of war" operates in a world which is certainly not ideal. Hence, the words of Glaucon unfortunately apply.

[15]The proscription of indirect support efforts is still viewed so conscienciously by neutral Sweden that, "Parliament decided that Sweden should not consider membership in the (European Economic) Community because the cooperation and coordination of foreign policy inside the Community is tantamount to that performed inside an alliance." Wachtmeister lecture.

[16]Dietrich Schindler, "State of War, Belligerency, and Armed Conflict" in Antonio Cassese, ed., The New Humanitarian Law of Armed Conflict (Napoli: Editoriale Scientifica, 1979), 3 and George Grafton Wilson, *Naval War College,*

different interpretations. In armed conflict such as insurrections and civil wars, respect for the laws of war, or the expectation of that respect, by states that found themselves so engaged, brought those laws into effect outside of the purely international construct.[17]

The essence of the law of neutrality, codified in the Hague Conventions, is impartiality. This expectation of impartiality by the neutrals was based on one thing: their desire to stay out of the war.[18] If their interests were involved in the war, states were expected to either become participants as belligerents or stand aside as a neutral and endure some damage to their interests to avoid the costs of war.

Neutrality certainly was not always viewed this way. Grotius saw war placing a demand on all states to serve justice and the responsibility to decide what course of action would best deliver that justice on their leaders. Therefore, in the early 17th century Grotius viewed the obligations of neutrals this way:

> It is the duty of those, who profess neutrality in a war to do nothing towards increasing the strength of a party maintaining an unjust cause, nor to impede the measures of a power engaged in a just and righteous cause . . . in doubtful cases

---

International Law Studies (ILS) V (Washington, DC: GPO, 1905), 171. See George Grafton Wilson, *ILS* VIII (1908), 117-255, for the texts of all conventions concluded at the Hague in 1907. For the effective conventions with their respective parties and reservations see Dietrich Schindler and Jiri Toman, eds., *The Laws of Armed Conflict*, rev. ed. (The Netherlands: Sijhoff and Noordhoff, 1981).

[17]"It is the policy of the United States to apply the law of armed conflict to all circumstances in which the armed forces of the United States are engaged in combat operations, regardless of whether such hostilities are declared or otherwise designated as 'war'." *The Commander's Handbook on the Law of Naval Operations, NWP 9* (Washington, DC: U.S. Navy Department, Office of the C.N.O., 1987), 27.

[18]"The rules laid down in the Hague Conventions are based on long experience of what should not be tolerated by belligerent states and may lead them to regard a neutral state as a legitimate target for countermeasures, maybe even war." Wachtmeister lecture.

they ought to show themselves impartial.[19]

In the centuries since, neutrality has come to be defined more narrowly.[20] States are now given the choice of joining the war or not acting on their assessment of justice. (States frequently choose an unacceptable middle path). This seems a submission to power politics, but it does discourage the spread of war to other states, inhibits self-righteous interference in the affairs of others, and reduces the problems inherent in subjective assessments of "justice."

A belligerent cannot be expected to tolerate third states assisting his enemy without taking action against them. The narrower law of neutrality permits a belligerent to take action short of war against those states that do not join the war but behave in an "unneutral" manner. This may take several forms ranging from mere tense silence through diplomatic protest to armed reprisal. If the belligerent decides that these actions would prove ineffective, it may resort to a declaration of war or simply commence hostilities against the "unneutral" state. The form of reaction to violations of neutral duties selected depends upon the aggrieved nation's political assessment of whether the exercise of belligerent rights will deter future unneutral behavior or cause the transgressor to join the fighting. In practice, this reflects the belligerent's cost-benefit analysis of dealing with an additional enemy as distinguished from an "unneutral neutral".[21]

As to the law of war at sea, unneutral service—that is,

---

[19]Hugo Grotius, *The Rights of War and Peace*, trans. A. C. Campbell (Washington, DC: M. Walter Dunn Publishing, 1901), Book III, Chap. XVII, II, 377.

[20]"In the fourteenth century Bartolus pointed out that each party would necessarily determine the justice of its own cause, and made the time-honored distinction between legal and ethical aspects of the problem and between war and reprisals. The word 'just' acquired so many meanings that it was of no legal use whatsoever." Edwin Borchard, "War, Neutrality and Non-Belligerency," *The American Journal of International Law* 35 (*AJIL*) (1941), 620.

[21]"Neutrality does not cease to exist if it is violated either by the neutral state not fulfilling all of its obligations or by violations perpetrated by a belligerent state." Wachtmeister lecture.

ignoring the neutral duty of impartiality—can stamp an individual vessel with hostile character. An unneutral vessel loses the protection afforded by neutrality to a degree roughly commensurate with the magnitude of its departure from impartiality. The ship could merely lose its contraband cargo or, in a more serious breach, could be taken into port and held over for adjudication in a Prize Court or, in the most extreme case, could even be destroyed.[22] This could happen if, for example, instead of heaving to when ordered by a belligerent warship—seeking to exercise its right of visit and search—the unneutral vessel attempted to flee or run a blockade.

The decision to assert additional belligerent rights (beyond visit and search) in response to unneutral acts is supported by the law, but it is a policy decision that must consider the tactical and political situation. The key question is, can the belligerent better afford the unneutral support of its enemy or the risk of another belligerent joining the war?[23]

During the time frame pertinent to this study, practice of states not complying with impartiality when neutrality was claimed was viewed as a departure from obligations, not as a reduction of the law's expectations.

---

[22]"Under the law of naval warfare, any merchant vessel, even under neutral flags, could become a legitimate military objective liable to attack and destruction due to the performance of certain acts, such as blockaderunning, refusal to stop, or resisting visit and search. Such civilian objects would then be treated like a combatant ship, without however being entitled to exercise belligerent rights like a man of war." Elmar Rauch, "The Protocol Additional to the Geneva Conventions for the Protection of Victims of International Armed Conflicts and the United Nations Convention on the Law of the Sea: Repercussions on the Law of Naval Warfare", Report to the Committee for the Protection of Human Life in Armed Conflict of the International Society for Military Law and Law of War, Bonn, Federal Republic of Germany, July 1983, 53.

[23]Hersh Lauterpacht, "The Limits of the Operation of the Law of War", *British Yearbook of International Law* 30 (BYBIL) (1953), 238; George Grafton Wilson, *ILS* XXV (1925), 74, 170; John Colombos, *International Law of the Sea*, 5th rev. ed. (London: Longmans, 1962), 589-590; Marjorie M. Whiteman, *Digest of International Law* 11, 180; Robert W. Tucker, *ILS* XLX (sic) (1955), 197, 199n, 258-259. See also Hans Kelsen, *ILS* XLIX (1954), 157 for a summary of neutral duties.

The 1907 Hague Conventions and the 1909 Declaration of London, crafted to strengthen the force of the law of neutrality, expected impartiality. Even though many states later chose to act in an unneutral manner during World War I, this behavior was not seen as changing the fundamental requirements of the law of neutrality laid down in the Hague Conventions.[24]

After the war, the Covenant of the League of Nations required states to take actions that in some cases seemed to make neutrality obsolete. But the Covenant bound only those states that became parties, and its sanctions were not applied in many cases—partly for lack of will and partly because the facts are never as clear as treaties assume.

The Convention on Maritime Neutrality was signed in Havana in 1928 and entered into force in 1931 (May 1932 for the United States). Its provisions still required impartiality of neutrals.[25]

---

[24]"It is true that at times a state has conceived that its interests might be better served by a course of action not in accord with international law, but such a condition has not been regarded in practice or in the courts as sufficient ground for setting aside accepted law or for proclaiming a purpose of following a policy at wide variance with international law though exceptional conditions have been from time to time admitted as ameliorating obligations.", George Grafton Wilson, *ILS* XXXIV (1934), 65. This also points out the difference between a state acting to serve its interests and one which is acting to preserve its rights. The latter finds far greater support in the law, of course—since law defines rights and politics defines interests.

The view of contemporary neutrality requirements is summarized for today's U.S. naval forces as:

"As a general rule of international law, all acts of hostility in neutral territory, including neutral lands, neutral waters, and neutral airspace, are prohibited. A neutral nation has the duty to prevent the use of its territory as a place of sanctuary or as a base of operations by belligerent forces of any side. If the neutral nation is unable or unwilling to enforce effectively its rights of inviolability, an aggrieved belligerent may resort to acts of hostility in neutral territory against enemy forces, including warships and military aircraft, making unlawful use of that territory." *NWP 9*, para. 7.3. *ILS* IX (1909) provides the text of the "Declaration of London" and some related documents.

[25]W. M. Malloy, *Treaties, Conventions, International Acts, Protocols and Agreements Between the United States of American and Other Powers 1976-1937* IV,4748; Schindler and Toman, 869; George Grafton Wilson, *ILS* XXXV (1935), 119.

The experience of World War I did have some effect on the attitudes of international lawyers. In 1936 George Grafton Wilson offered the opinion, "An imperfect war might have as a corollary an imperfect neutrality."[26] This might have alluded to some future exception but did not reflect contemporary acceptance of a legally defined "imperfect neutral."

As World War II became an inevitability, the pragmatic appeal of the protection offered by impartiality removed any ambiguities of interpretation, and attitudes were less speculative about the options available to avowed neutrals. In 1939, Payton Sibley Wild, Jr., wrote, "At the core of neutrality lies impartiality" and admitted "Any sort of unneutral conduct does open the way for reprisals by the injured belligerent."[27]

While the law may have remained unchanged, the paradox persisted. Strictly impartial neutrality was an inherently illogical choice of the powerful nation whose interests were threatened— but the cause of peace is sometimes best served by keeping the more powerful nations out of war. A powerful nation should have an option to protect its interests other than by becoming a belligerent and escalating the war, but the law persists unchanged, no matter how difficult it might be to comply with. Impartial neutrality, under the law, expects a state to "surrender certain rights not worth fighting for and prepare to fight for others . . . too vital to surrender."[28] At the same time, however, the neutral state is required to defend its own territory, with force if necessary, against unneutral use by belligerents, even a belligerent it considers just (or might otherwise favor). Failing to deny such use of its territory gives rise to the right of reprisal in the offending belligerent's opponent. This presents yet another paradox because, at least in the eyes of some, "It would be the supreme folly to go to war to maintain your right to stay out of

---

[26]George Grafton Wilson, *ILS* XXXVI (1936), 83.

[27]Payton Sibley Wild, Jr., *ILS* XXXIX (1939), 9, 55. This opinion was also offered: " ... the neutral state in so far as it is represented by the official acts of its government, must refrain from giving any direct assistance to either belligerent in the prosecution of the war." Charles G. Fenwick, *American Neutrality: Trial and Failure* (New York: New York University Press, 1940), 106.

[28]Fenwick, v.

war."[29] But staying out of war is not the right in question; sovereignty itself is violated if neutral territory is used by a belligerent to support its war aims. If such a violation goes unanswered, sovereignty could soon be at risk on a variety of counts.

Pragmatic evaluation reveals this dilemma will not be resolved by committing illogical acts but by assessing national interests. When the costs of being neutral no longer make sense, the time has arrived to abandon neutrality no matter how distasteful or dangerous this might prove, and this course of action was followed repeatedly by the United States.

Further, in today's world there is an expectation within the United States, and outside as well—at least among friendly states—that the United States will act in pursuit of justice even at the expense of impartiality. As was mentioned, however, in the past the imperatives dictating such partial actions were not always accompanied by a decision, an acknowledgment, or perhaps even a realization that the protections of neutrality were abandoned in the process. Therein lies the problem for naval forces. When change can be so subtle, will naval commanders be astute enough, or even well enough informed of events, to recognize when the United States might be perceived by belligerents as abandoning neutrality (or violating neutral obligations), whether that reflects intentions or not? This is critical because, as noted earlier, the perception of U.S. actions by the contending belligerents may change the tactical environment in which the ships operate.

This gray area of proclaimed neutrality and practice perceived as unneutral raises a question regarding legal labels, which might be inconsequential except that states apply them as a matter of policy when they want the legal results to flow from those labels. So, in what category are states that claim to be neutral yet, as a matter of national policy, or perceived national policy, perform unneutral acts or fail to fulfill their neutral duties? Before World War II, Professor Wild claimed these states were in a condition of "qualified neutrality."[30] The law gave them no name.

---

[29]Ibid., 3.
[30]Wild, *ILS* XXXIX (1939), 54.

At the beginning of World War II, the dilemma of the legal requirements of neutrality was recognized by those states not prepared to take action to stop aggression. The dangers of impartiality as the essence of neutrality were the source of such denunciations as this:

> Neutrality in the traditional sense of treating both sides alike meant in practice making no distinction between right and wrong. Neutrality was the negation of law and order; it was the product of international anarchy; it was contrary to the fundamental concepts of law and order.[31]

But who was to impose this order the law required? The belligerents would enforce it against neutrals and the neutrals against the belligerents. Law did not require any state to abstain from action against wrongdoers, but if it chose neutrality, a state was legally required to do so without exerting any direct or indirect influence in favor of one belligerent of the other. Pragmatically, this was the price neutrals paid for being spared by the wrongdoer, that is, retaining the protections the law afforded a neutral.

If a weak state took up a position of neutrality it was understandable, if not wise. In a sense, weak neutrals were gambling that an aggressor state would not eventually turn on them. If a powerful state remained neutral the situation was less easily understood. It might be that the situation was not clear as to which state was wrong. This is not an easy determination to make (and could account for some cases of weak state neutrality as well). But when a powerful state could determine an aggressor to its own satisfaction, and its interests in international peace, stability, and security were threatened by a successful aggression, the criticism leveled by Professor Fenwick above seems justified.

In fact, neutrality did not contribute to anarchy. Despite what

---

[31]Fenwick, 30. Also, "The freedom of states to remain aloof from unjust demands upon their neighbors, to recognize fruits of aggression, though tolerated by traditional international law, accords a legal protection to war . . . difficult to reconcile with principles of justice," Wright, 210.

they considered a just cause that might be damaged by their neutrality, states deciding on neutrality were choosing in essence expediency over justice (or at least their own short term over long-term national interests). Neutrality was being used as a legal cloak for self-serving policy and was being blamed for perceived moral deficiencies of the true policy. The problem here is more deep seated than the law of neutrality being used as a shield for true intentions—the entire law of war is drawn into question: "Given a system in which war is no illegality it ineluctably follows that victorious war must be allowed to change rights."[32] Boundaries will be moved, governments will be changed, countries will cease to exist, and people will be subjected to a new system of national laws when wars are won.[33] When war is undertaken for aggressive purposes, those results are often not just. This problem was addressed by Grotius, the League of Nations Covenant, the Kellogg-Briand Pact, and the Charter of the United Nations—and it has not yet been solved.

The tradeoff accepted by impartial neutrality when war is precipitated by aggression is the preservation of peace at the potential expense of justice,[34] but what is a state to do when it is not prepared to become a belligerent? Remember, the law of

---

[32]R. Y. Jennings, *The Acquisition of Territory in International Law* (New York: Oceana, 1963), 52.

[33]"In spite of the prohibition on the use of force in the Charter of the United Nations, it is still possible, in certain cases for force to produce juridicial effects: for example, acquisitions made by the victor after a war, the independence of colonies, the secession of States, such secession being subsequently recognized by the mother country." *ICJ Rep.*, 1949 (Corfu Channel Case—Individual Opinion of Judge Alvarez), 42-43.

[34]"By treaty the use of force is forbidden in international affairs and 'justice' is to be rendered by . . . the United Nations, set up to do the job free of local passions. . . . If 'justice' cannot be done, the law prizes stability, security, life, property and other things more highly; 'justice' is a problem for heaven, beyond the capacity of man . . . the rules of law focus on the problem of limiting the conflict, not of winning it for one 'just' party or the other. Those rules require that states choose between belligerency, in which case their property becomes a legitimate target of the 'enemy', and 'neutrality', in which case they may not help even the 'just' side, but are bound to treat both sides as legal equals." Alfred P. Rubin, "Support for Warring Nation Removes Any Claim of 'Neutrality'", *Boston Herald*, 10 June 1984, 51:1-2.

neutrality codified at The Hague demands impartiality and can even require the use of armed force against a belligerent (including one which is the victim of aggression) should the belligerent violate the neutral's territorial jurisdiction in contravention of the law.[35]

From this perspective we must consider Quincy Wright as having a cynical but correct view of the world when he wrote: "Neutrality is, in fact, the policy which all states, particularly those with maritime commercial interests, have tried to achieve in the balance of power system. To be able to remain neutral is to hold the balance of power."[36] Wright assesses the power relationship and its pragmatic logic, ignoring both the overarching principle of justice the law should serve and the moral underpinnings without which it will collapse. Even states looking for short-term solutions must recognize that their legal claims must admit reciprocity, as they, too, may become legal victims of such law.

Another view sees states without significant power seeking refuge in the law of neutrality, in the hope they may be spared until they are prepared to confront the aggressor successfully. Some might abstain from joining the war as a belligerent in the sometimes false hope the war might end better if its intensity is not increased. States could reasonably fear entry into the war would only start a chain reaction of other states aligning on either side, making peace more difficult to attain and vastly increasing the potential for death and destruction.

The decision to become an active belligerent is by no means simple; in addition to the considerations outlined above, the role of neutral states during war is not only important, it may be essential—neutrals can be an anchor against the tide of violence. When a neutral can afford true impartiality it can act as a voice of reason, bringing a detached objectivity to the situation that the belligerents embroiled in the conflict can never hope to provide themselves. A true neutral can lead the way back to the peace in

---

[35]"A neutral state using armed resistance to stave off an intruder must not, in accordance with international law, be regarded as having committed a hostile act." Wachtmeister lecture.

[36]Wright, 135.

the role of mediator, or at least slow the spread and diminish the horror of war, in part by acting as protecting powers for the victims of war as envisaged by the 1949 Geneva Conventions.[37]

Each state entering a war raises the stakes the war is being fought for—and, therefore, the means belligerents will use to assure victory or prevent defeat. Professor Daniel P. O'Connell explains:

> Before international law has been discounted there has always been a graduated escalation of the war to the point where no important neutrals stand aloof from the conflict, and the military situation has become so desperate that limitations on the conduct of operations have ceased to be of persuasive value or political importance.[38]

In this instance the law is imperfect, being unable to prevent aggression while preserving restraint against aggressors, and thus many conclude it would be best if the balance-of-power system were subjugated to an international security organization mandating a collective security arrangement. Indeed, this was a basic motivation for the creation of both the League of Nations and the United Nations, and many believe the Covenant and, later, the Charter caused the law of neutrality to be revised to

---

[37]Department of State, *United States Treaties and Other International Acts* (TIAS) (Washington: Department of State, 1939), 3362, UST 6, 3114-3216, (Convention I: Geneva Convention for the Amelioration of the Condition of the Wounded and Sick in the Armed Forces in the Field) (Washington, DC: Department of State, 1939-); TIAS 3363, UST 6, 3217-3315, (Convention II: Geneva Convention for the Amelioration of the Wounded, Sick and Shipwrecked Members of the Armed Forces at Sea); TIAS 3364, UST 6, 3316-3515, (Convention III: Geneva Convention Relative to the Treatment of Prisoners of War); TIAS 3365, UST 6, 3516-3695, (Convention IV: Geneva Convention Relative to the Protection of Civilian Persons in Time of War) all dated 12 August 1949. Also in Schindler and Toman, 305-331, 333-354, 355-425, and 427-488, respectively, and 299-523 inclusive for the attendant documents and listings of reservations by the parties. See especially TIAS 3362, 3363, and 3364, Article 8, in each of the Conventions and TIAS 3365, Article 9, regarding Protecting Powers.

[38]D. P. O'Connell, *The Influence of Law on Sea Power* (Annapolis: Naval Institute Press, 1975), 50-51.

allow discriminating and discriminatory neutrality as the norm—much as Grotius described the duties of a neutral above. (This philosophy can only become effective, however, if the international security organization is both empowered and disposed to perform its intended role).

NEUTRALITY AND CIVIL WAR

The laws of war and neutrality replace (or come into operation with) the law of peace whenever hostilities occur, even in internal conflicts.[39] The applicability of the laws of war and neutrality to internal conflicts, however, is not universally accepted, because bringing this law into force places restrictions upon the incumbent government and grants entitlements to the rebel forces. Most governments would prefer to deal with rebels as criminals under domestic law—treating them as belligerents makes their killing of government forces a belligerent right and severely complicates the incumbent government's options. Should the conflict take on an international character, however, the law of neutrality can apply to some of the legal questions which arise. [40] Both the decisionmaking process and the ability to consider the United States neutral in these situations generally conform to the situation described for international conflicts above.

The situation has been clarified somewhat by the Geneva Conventions of 1949. Article 2 of each convention is identical and holds they apply to all "international" armed conflicts whether considered to be war by all the participants or not. Article 3 extends certain protections even when the war is not of an international character and entreats the parties to the Conventions to attempt to have their provisions to apply as

---

[39]Tucker, 183n and 201-202; Roscoe Ralph Oglesby, *Internal War and the Search for Normative Order* (The Hague: Martinus Nijhoff, 1971), 105, 119; Schindler, 4-5, 6, 13.

[40]See Rubin, "The Concept of Neutrality in International Law" for a discussion of the evolution of U.S. neutrality legislation, especially 366-371.

broadly as possible to the conflict.[41] These conventions apply, however, only to the humanitarian aspects of the law of war and treat the subject of neutrality tangentially.[42] It is notable that they acknoweldge that neutrals will exist, indicating the parties to these treaties believed the status of neutrality had *not* been superseded by events or other treaties.

When an insurgent group has achieved the level of control over territory, support from the population, or influence over interests of other states, resulting in their receiving the diplomatic support of other states, they are normally recognized as "belligerents," and, "In the absence of an international consensus as to the legal status of a rebel group every government coming to a view . . . may be entitled to . . . choose the label (bandit, *de facto* regime, government, etc.) which best suits its policy."[43]

When the label attached is "belligerent" (or something even closer to a new government), the legal consequence is that the insurgent group will be regarded as a legal person under international law.[44] Those who recognize these "belligerents" also assume responsibilities regarding them under the laws of war and neutrality. As will be seen, the "recognition" may be tacit or implied and even flow from actions inconsistent with declared government policy.[45] Ambivalence, domestic political

---

[41]Op. cit. note 2:37. See also Alfred P. Rubin, "Reagan's Error About Lieut. Goodman's Status", *The New York Times*, 30 December 1983, A22:3-5; for a practical example of the law of war operating to provide protections even while the United States denied "war" existed.

[42]"The reluctance to admit gaps in the applicability of the Conventions has resulted in what seems an excessive reliance on the precise terms of Conventions to define the legal situation in armed conflicts." Alfred P. Rubin, "The Status of Rebels Under the Geneva Conventions of 1949", International and Comparative Law Quarterly 21 (1972), 483.

[43] Rubin, "Rebels", 475.

[44]"When the drawing of legal results depends upon the attaching of legal labels, the decision whether or not the label properly attaches becomes a question of law and subject to differing opinions. Since opinions may differ, the decision as to adopting one opinion or another becomes a question of state policy." "Rebels", 474.

[45]"The penetrating analysis of Chief Justice Taft as Arbitrator in the *Tinoco Arbitration* of 1923, arguing that 'recognition' meant only what the 'recognizing' state intended it to mean, and that nonrecognition could be legally irrelevant regardless of its political utility, applies equally to the state of war

considerations, lack of understanding, and duplicity may individually or collectively cloud the issue of recognition.[46] Such recognition should not be given lightly, however, because just the *granting* of such recognition can have legal consequences for the recognizing state:

> Recognizing or treating a rebellious regime as the successor government while the previously recognized regime is still in control constitutes unlawful interference in the internal affairs of that state. If recognition or acceptance of the rebellious regime is accompanied by military support, it may violate Article 2 (4) of the United Nations Charter as a use or threat of force against the political independence of the other state. It is lawful, however, for a state to recognize the authority of an insurgent group over territory within its control, to give effect to measures by such a group that affect the rights of foreign nationals within that territory, and to deal with it in limited ways as a belligerent.[47]

So, the internal war situation can be viewed in two ways, both of which have the same legal, and perhaps tactical, result:

• Once the war takes on an international character through an international consensus supporting or recognizing the authority of the insurgents, states have a responsibility to the incumbent government to behave as neutrals or risk countermeasures.

• Unlawful interference in the state's internal affairs may be claimed if the war remains entirely internal, and support or recognition of the force opposing the government is premature (for example, by a single state's policy decision prior to international consensus). The government of the aggrieved state

---

regardless of the preference of lawyers for clear categories and rules." Rubin, "The Law of War", 140.

[46]J. L. Brierly, *The Law of Nations,* 6th ed. (Oxford: Oxford University Press, 1963), 142; William W. Bishop, Jr., *International Law: Cases and Materials,* 3rd ed. (Boston: Little, Brown & Co., 1971), 393; and H. Lauterpacht, *Recognition in International Law* (Cambridge: Cambridge University Press, 1948), 270, also digested in Bishop at 395-396. See also John Norton Moore, ed., *Law & Civil War in the Modern World* (Baltimore: The Johns Hopkins University Press, 1974), passim.

[47]*Rest. 3rd,* 203, Comment g, 1:86.

in this case may consider the same set of potential countermeasures and policy options as when there is an international consensus regarding the belligerency (or international character of the conflict).

The two situations would then find the business of dealing with the rebels a violation of either neutral obligations or the obligation to refrain from interfering in the internal affairs of the state involved—but the dangers to naval forces resulting from unneutral behavior or interference are identical. Further, the logic that will likely guide policy decisions remains the same.

The results also flow if the "intervention" consists of support for the embattled incumbent government after the rebels achieve a degree of success sufficient to make it clear that there is a struggle for authenticity or legitimacy going on. Either neutral obligations in a state of belligerency would be violated, or the support of one faction against another all in a single state would amount to an intervention in that state's internal affairs. Either categorization would justify countermeasures, including the use of force by the faction aggrieved by the interfering unneutral state.

While support to either an embattled government or a favored insurgent group may prove a suitable alternative to policy makers, both involve legal (and attendant practical) consequences that could alter the tactical situation for naval forces in the area and that must not be ignored.

2.
THE CHANGE

*The intercourse . . . steadily increasing between the
nations of the earth, has now extended so enormously
that a violation of right in one portion of the world is
felt all over it.*[1]

THE BEGINNING

The change from mainland expansionism to worldwide interests
and influence came to the United States in the final decade of the
19th century. On 16 January 1893,[2] U.S. citizens residing in
Hawaii became involved in a plot to seize power from the royal
family and were saved from themselves by the U.S. Minister in
the islands, John L. Stevens, when their so-called insurgency was
about to be crushed by the native Hawaiians. *U.S.S. BOSTON*
was in Honolulu harbor at the time; Stevens requested that her
Commanding Officer land troops to prevent bloodshed. A
provisional government was established, and Queen Liliuokalani
was dethroned when 164 sailors and Marines arrived at the gates
of the royal palace. Minister Stevens, without proper authority

---

[1]Emmanuel Kant quoted in Inis L. Claude, Jr., *Swords into Plowshares: The
Problems and Progress of International Organizations* (New York: Random
House, 1971), 251 from Emmanuel Kant, Perpetual Peace, trans. (New York:
Liberal Arts Press, 1948), 21.

[2]"A Revolution in Hawaii", *The New York Times*, 29 January 1893, 1:6-2:7.
See also Kenneth J. Hagan, *This People's Navy: The Making of American
Seapower* (New York: The Free Press, 1991), 201-203.

recognized the insurrectionists (who had escaped defeat through his humanitarian actions) as the government and established a U.S. protectorate. The protectorate was proclaimed by the U.S. Minister on 1 February, a mere two weeks later. By mid-month a proposed annexation treaty was delivered to Washington by one British and four U.S. citizens who presented themselves as "Hawaiians." According to diplomatic historian Thomas Bailey, newly elected President Cleveland would have none of it and attempted to restore the Queen to the throne; she, however, quickly pledged to have the heads of the insurrectionists. Although the annexation treaty remained intolerable, Cleveland's ethics succumbed to domestic political considerations—no president could restore a sovereign intent on butchering his constituents.[3]

Consideration of the problem lingered for years. In 1897, when it became clear the Japanese wanted to annex Hawaii, the issue moved closer to resolution. Captain Alfred Thayer Mahan, the noted naval strategist, and others argued that Hawaii in Japanese hands posed a threat to the Pacific coast of the United States. Annexation was finally precipitated by the Spanish-American War in 1898. The *de facto* insurrectionist government compromised its neutrality to support the United States' effort to resupply Admiral Dewey and support the transport of troops destined for the conquest of Manila. This sacrifice of neutrality in favor of the United States became part of the rationale for annexation when the U.S. Government finally ended a half decade of ambivalence and debate.[4]

---

[3]Moore, I: 495-510, and Thomas A. Bailey, *A Diplomatic History of the American People*, 10th ed. (Englewood Cliffs, N.J.: Prentice Hall, Inc., 1980), 428-433.

[4]Joint Resolution for the Annexation of Hawaii, *U.S. Statutes at Large* (*USStat*) 30, 750-751; Bailey, 433-435; Robert Seager II and Doris D. Maguire, eds., *Letters and Papers of Alfred Thayer Mahan* (Annapolis: Naval Institute Press, 1975), see letter to James H. Kyle, Senator from South Dakota, dated 4 February 1898 from the 55th Cong., 2nd Sess., Senate Reports No. 681, 99 quoted at II:538-539; Henry Steele Commager, ed., *Documents of American*

Other questions regarding neutrality played important roles in this momentous time of national transition for the United States.[5]

THE SPANISH-AMERICAN WAR

The United States tried in vain to avoid involvement in the civil war ravaging the Spanish colony of Cuba as it sought independence from Madrid. An activist press and an adventurous populace combined to place the United States a bit too close to

---

History, 3rd ed. (New York: F. S. Crofts & Co., 1947) also contains the Joint Resolution that annexed Hawaii at II:186-187, doc. 348. Commager's introductory comments to the document acknowledges that the U.S. use of the islands as a naval base during the Spanish-American War was a factor in the determination to annex them. See Thomas J. Osborne, *"Empire Can Wait": American Opposition to Hawaiian Annexation, 1893-1898* (Kent, Ohio: Kent State University Press, 1981), 115 and 159n for and interesting summary of the final Senate debates regarding this aspect of the matter. It is noteworthy that the Senate documents regarding the discussion of Hawaii's compromised neutrality remained classified SECRET until 1969. Whether this was because of sensitivity or inertia is unknown.

[5]It is worth noting that an incident related to those dealt with in the following analysis happened in October of 1891. The United States was concerned for the safety and security of U.S. citizens and property in Chile during their civil war. A number of warships visited Chilean waters during the civil war and *U.S.S. BALTIMORE* was in Valparaiso harbor when the fighting ended. Two *BALTIMORE* sailors died in a riot in which they were attacked because they wore the U.S. Navy uniform and were seen as aligned with the deposed (and despised) government. The United States had treated the incumbent government as legitimate during the war and the insurgents were not treated as belligerents. Therefore, U.S. behavior was clearly not impartial. When the insurgents succeeded to power clear animosity prevailed. The way in which the riot was handled in Chilean courts and in diplomatic exchanges almost resulted in war with the United States. Subsequent events involved the harassment of *U.S.S. YORKTOWN* in Valpariso harbor. This may be the first incident in which U.S. sailors died because of unneutral behavior by the United States. For an insightful, detailed, and well documented account of what happened to *BALTIMORE* and her crew, see Joyce S. Goldberg, *The BALTIMORE Affair* (Lincoln & London: University of Nebraska Press, 1986).

the vortex of the dissolving Spanish Empire. The government maintained an appropriate public policy but did little to prevent support to the insurgents who kept an informal, but very effective financial and logistic support infrastructure operating out of New York City under the guidance of Cuban hero Jose Martí. Indeed, private U.S. citizens became deeply involved in both the financial and operational aspects of the revolution.[6]

One of the earliest and most notorious incidents involved the U.S. flag sidewheeler *VIRGINIUS*. In October 1873, *VIRGINIUS* was involved in landing rebels and arms when a Spanish warship, *TORNADO*, interfered. A pursuit ensued that ended within sight of refuge in the British waters of Jamaica. The American prize was taken to Cuba, where the captain, crew, and passengers were sentenced to death and executed. The incident—despite *VIRGINIUS* covertly but notoriously belonging to the Cuban Junta—almost took the United States to war with Spain over the seizure of an "American" ship on the high seas.[7]

The pattern continued essentially unabated. U.S. citizens were also funding Martí's efforts when he died in Cuba in May 1895, a few short weeks after he went ashore to join in the insurgents'

---

[6]While precise determination is not possible because states are entitled to auto-interpret the requirements of the law respected publicists on the subject would likely agree, "it is probably correct that in its essence the law of neutrality fixes obligations on a state but not directly on its nationals." Rubin, "The Concept of Neutrality in International Law", 372-373. Professor Rubin has also made the point, in a personal note to the author on an earlier draft of this work, that: "On the other hand, the failure of the United States to control these individuals was probably a violation of international law about which Spain could properly complain, and did. The U.S. Neutrality Act of 1794 was almost certainly violated by the American supporters of Cuban rebels."

[7]See G. J. A. O'Toole, *The Spanish War: An American Epic 1898* (New York: W. W. Norton & Co., Inc, 1984) and Claude Julien, *America's Empire*, trans., (New York: Pantheon Books, 1974) especially 39-44. Coincidentally, both ships involved had served the Confederacy as blockade runners in the War Between the States.

fight directly.[8] A variety of actions by private citizens, who could not be, or were not, restrained by the U.S. government, and seemingly endless agitation by domestic newspapers severely strained relations with Spain.

After a riot in Havana there was great concern over the safety of U.S. citizens and their property in Cuba. A stabilizing influence was sought. In January of 1898, the battleship *MAINE* was sent to Havana, in an effort to impress the importance of this concern upon the Spanish colonial government.[9] The mission was unstated and never alluded to during the various calls made by Captain Charles D. Sigsbee, *MAINE*'s Commanding Officer. Regardless of its subtlety, no one was confused about the message delivered by the "friendly" visit of this warship that arrived without notice. As history has recorded, the ship and many of her crew were to remain in Cuba for the rest of their lives.

The loss of the battleship *MAINE* is popularly cited as the reason for the war with Spain,[10] but the blatantly partiality of the United States undoubtedly contributed to the conflict. By the time *MAINE* blew up, the relationship with Spain had degraded sufficiently to make the idea of sabotage by the Spanish all too credible.   Analysis of information more clearly understood with hindsight indicates the ship actually may have destroyed herself.

---

[8]Mentioned in Louis Morton, General Editor, *The MacMillan Wars of the United States*, David F. Trask, *The War With Spain in 1898* (New York & London: MacMillan & Collier, 1981), 2-3. In more detail in O'Toole, 48-51. Later, in November 1895, the United States arrested the captain and officers of the Danish steamer *HORSA* for transporting a group of rebels from a rendezvous off the coast of New Jersey to Cuba. They were found guilty of filibustering. See O'Toole, 60.

[9]"*MAINE* Sent to Cuba", *The New York Times*, 25 January 1898, 1:7-2:2.

[10]"*MAINE* Blown Up", *The New York Times*, 16 February 1898, 1:7-2:1. The event is covered extensively by O'Toole, Trask, James C. Bradford, ed., *Crucible of Empire* (Annapolis: Naval Institute Press, 1993), and Elbert J. Benton, *International Law and Diplomacy of the Spanish-American War* (Baltimore: Johns Hopkins Press), 1908.

Experiences of similar ships at the time indicate that bituminous coal in one of *MAINE*'s bunkers likely ignited through spontaneous combustion. Such a fire would transmit deadly heat directly to an ammunition magazine through a shared bulkhead, causing an explosion sufficient to destroy *MAINE*. It is unlikely that anyone will ever conclusively prove how the explosion really occurred. The United States assumed the Spanish were at fault, believing Spain was motivated to take such drastic action because of the interference of the United States and U.S. citizens in the civil war.[11]

The war that ensured involved actions that stretched halfway around the world. Commodore Dewey's campaign against the

---

[11]For well researched discussions of the events which led to the war and its conduct see O'Toole, supra note 7. Regarding the cause of the explosion which destroyed *MAINE* see H. G. Rickover, *How the Battleship MAINE Was Destroyed* (Washington: Naval History Division, Department of the Navy, 1976). Admiral Rickover's study concluded that an internal explosion was likely the cause and offered some theories for how it might have occurred. This conclusion is interesting when compared to the contemporary reporting such as "Destruction of Warship *MAINE* was the Work of an Enemy" and "Naval Officers Think *MAINE* was Destroyed by Spanish Mine" both running across all columns of the first page of *The New York Journal and Advertizer*, 17 February 1898. On the same front page were repeated notices that William Randolph Hearst was prepared to pay a $50,000 reward for the identity of the perpetrator. Worth pondering is an envelope from a Ward Line steamer in the U.S. Naval Academy Museum. Written in pencil on the envelope is the following:

"Forsyth, Key West

Tell Admiral *MAINE* blown up and destroyed. Send Light House tenders. Many killed and wounded. **Don't send war vessels if others available.** (emphasis added)

/s/Sigsbee"

The envelope was given to newspaperman George B. Rea to take ashore and transmit the message to Commander James M. Forsyth who was the Commander of the Naval Station at Key West, for relay to the Admiral who was Rear Admiral Montgomery Sicard, Commander North Atlantic. Why was the Commanding Officer of the ship destroyed moments earlier urging his superior not to send warships? The answer will likely never be known, but it certainly does not lead one to believe Sigsbee felt his ship had been attacked.

Spanish forces in the Philippines, which, oddly enough, compromised Hawaiian neutrality, came as part of the effort to free Cuba. Dewey far outmatched and easily defeated the Spanish Fleet at Manila Bay but likely could not have sustained his forces for long if the Hawaiian Islands had not served as a logistics base for U.S. naval forces in Asian waters. Hawaii also facilitated the reinforcement of Dewey's ships by Army troops. After defeating the Spanish and accepting their surrender, Dewey spent a period in which he did not have sufficient forces to occupy the city he had just conquered; army troops needed to come from the United States to make that a reality. Meanwhile, Dewey was doing a superb if tenuous job of maintaining a blockade in Manila Bay. The neutral British had denied Dewey's forces access to, and support from, Hong Kong, even to the extent of not permitting the use of telegraph facilities.[12]

Before long Dewey found a superior German fleet at his back. The German naval force failed to respect Dewey's blockade of Manila Bay, and on more than one occasion U.S. warships fired across the bows of their German counterparts before the Germans would heave to or even identify themselves. The Germans were intent on seizing bases in the Philippine Islands for themselves, specifically in Mindanao, and this

---

[12]"Dewey's Big Victory: Dewey's Victory at Manila Bay and Report", *The New York Times*, 8 May 1898, 1:2-2:6. For a good summary of the naval aspects of the war see Frank Uhlig, Jr., *How Navies Fight: The U.S. Navy and Its Allies* (Annapolis: Naval Institute, 1994), 61-74 especially 61-64 concerning the situation at Manila. For a thorough discussion of the issues of international law during the period including the latter phases of the insurrection and the subsequent war with Spain see *ILS* I (1901), Appendix 139-180, and Benton, passim.

eventually became an important factor in the U.S. decision to annex the Philippines.[13]   Puerto Rico, Cuba, and Guam had

---

[13]For a somewhat subjective, but firsthand, account of these events see George Dewey, *Autobiography of George Dewey: Admiral of the Navy*, reprint (Annapolis: Naval Institute Press, 1987), 223-231. See *USStat* 30, 1754 for the Treaty of Peace with Spain of 10 December 1898, also in Commager, *Documents*, II:187-189, doc. 349. Also Margaret Leech, *In the Days of McKinley* (New York: Harper & Brothers, 1959), 342-343 for peace treaty negotiations regarding the purchase of the Philippines. Cf. Bailey, 468-474. See also Holger H. Herwig, *Politics of Frustration: The United States in German Naval Planning, 1889-1941* (Boston: Little, Brown & Co., 1976), 29-32. Herwig's book is a well researched account of the relationship between Germany's war efforts and U.S. policy which relies upon original documents from the German archives. Time, access, and the ability to translate were not available to replicate his research, therefore it is relied upon as authoritative herein.   Herwig offers an insightful review of the issues involved in the confrontation between Commodore Dewey and Vice Admiral von Diederichs and their impact. The situation was so tense it allegedly precipitated a telegram from President McKinley to his naval commander in the Caribbean urging caution as hostilities with Germany were "imminent."

Historian David Trask, supra note 8, 378-381, discusses the incidents with the Germans and dismisses them as a misunderstanding between Dewey and Vice-Admiral von Dietrichs which turned on the question of the German refusing the right of visit being exercised against a neutral warship while Dewey was asserting the right to communicate with all vessels entering a blockaded port. Trask concludes that both flag officers eventually accepted the other's point of view and the rest of the story is myth. That said, Trask recounts the officers communicating through reciprocal visits by their aides (Lieutenant Thomas M. Brumby paid Dewey's call on the German) and documents that Dewey, in anger, told the Germans he would go to war to ensure his country's rights.

Another first hand account, Joseph L. Stickney, *Admiral Dewey at Manila and the Complete Story of the Philippines* (Philadelphia: J.H. Moore Co., 1899), 87-93, makes it clear that Dewey asked if the Germans were at war with the United States so that he might comply with his obligations as such. Stickney was also an aide to Dewey. Like Trask he cites events both at Manila and at Subic Bay in which the German behavior seemed to ignore the force of the publicized American blockade. An interesting departure is that Trask contends that there was concern the Filipinos wanted to ask for a German Prince to rule the islands while Stickney explains that Dewey's concern was the warm

come under U.S. rule when the armistice was signed in August of 1898, but the United States was still unsure about its appropriate role in the Philippines. National sentiment was ambivalent. Spain was seen as despotic, but the United States wanted to avoid an imperialist label.

When the peace treaty was signed in Paris that December, Cuba was freed, much to the chagrin of the Spanish who would have preferred to lose it to the United States, and the Philippines were purchased from Spain for $20 million. The United States was now a world power responsible for island empires in the Caribbean and the Pacific and far-flung interests associated with them. The impact of this on the character of the nation was not so subtle as to be unnoticed.[14]

THE CHANGE IS UNDERSTOOD

At the Hague Peace Conference in 1899, Captain Mahan, according to Barbara Tuchman's account, believed "What had been good for the United States as a weak neutral . . . would no longer be good for her as a Great Power. . . . He looked ahead to the rights of the belligerent rather than back to the rights of the neutral."[15]

It appears Mahan understood the impact of the new role the United States had undertaken, and it didn't take long before the

---

relations with the Spaniards whose fleet Dewey had recently destroyed.

In any case, it is clear that Dewey was operating beyond the limits of his lines of communications and had already spent some of his ammunition and coal. For the time being he was essentially unsupported and had not yet defeated or occupied the city. The Germans needed a coaling station in the Philippines. Their forces were continuing to grow in number and were not acknowledging Dewey's authority to his satisfaction. Dewey apparently approached the situation with more courage than strategic advantage!

[14]See *USStat* 30, 1754 for the Treaty of Peace with Spain of 10 December 1898, also in Commager, II:187-189, doc. 349.

[15]Barbara Tuchman, *The Proud Tower* (New York: MacMillan, 1966), 260. See also Seager and Maguire, letter to Admiral Sir John A. Fisher dated 18 July 1899, II:643-644.

international responsibilities inherent in new and some long-standing U.S. policies became clear to everyone else.

As an example, in February of 1904 the Hague Court of Permanent Arbitration gave precedence over other creditor nations to the states that used armed force to extract payment of debts from Venezuela in 1902,[16] thus offering new incentives to states who would use force to collect debts. During the Venezuela crisis, the United States imposed itself as a shield between those creditor nations and Venezuela, to uphold the Monroe Doctrine. The world economy, especially in much of the Western Hemisphere, was not well. If the United States were not to ignore extra-hemispheric interference and forsake the interests that gave birth to the doctrine, it likely would confront creditor nations attempting to collect payment by force more frequently in the future, or would somehow have to guarantee payment of other nations' debts. The United States chose the latter course. The result was the Roosevelt Corollary to the Monroe Doctrine that sent Navy and Marine Corps units throughout Latin America establishing and protecting U.S.-operated customs houses that supervised the international trade relations of debtor states, to keep the United States out of European wars.[17] Some have alleged this effort was a brand of imperialism and the trappings and temporary results bore this interpretation out. These

---

[16]Malloy, I:1872-1881 award at 1878-1881.

[17] James D. Richardson, ed., *A Compilation of the Messages and Papers of the Presidents 1789-1897*, XV (Washington, DC: By the Authority of the Congress, 1909), 6894-6930, for Roosevelt's Fourth Annual Message of 6 December 1904 especially 6923-6924; 6973-7023 for Roosevelt's Fifth Annual Message of 5 December 1905 especially 6995-6996; see also Commager, II:213-215, doc. 362, for Roosevelt's rationale for the corollary in his Annual Messages of 1904 and 1905; Samuel Flagg Bemis, *The Latin American Policy of the United States* (New York: Harcourt, Brace & Co., 1943), 151n; see also Whitney T. Perkins, *Constraint of Empire: The United States and Caribbean Interventions* (Westport, CN: Greenwood Press, 1981) passim; and, for a Venezuelan view of the 1902 debt crisis and blockade, see Miriam (*Sra. Blanco Fombona de*) Hood, *Gunboat Diplomacy 1895-1905: Great Power Pressure in Venezuela* (Winchester, Massachusetts: Allen & Unwin, Inc., 1983).

temporary protectorates were not sought as prizes, however; intervention was simply the lesser of two evils.[18] Indeed, there was so little profit to be made in these ventures that the Department of State had problems convincing private U.S. bankers to underwrite the foreign debts.

THE MEXICAN REVOLUTION
Taft Confronts Madero

Foreign investment had dominated the Mexican economy and foreign policy for decades. The unscrupulous behavior of the regime of Porfirio Diaz included seizing Indian land holdings and embezzling federal funds. Mexico was overdue for revolution by the time Diaz' government began to recognize that its control of the country might be challenged in 1910. Much of the foreign investment in Mexico at the time was in the form of enormous land holdings of U.S. citizens. Further, citizens of the United States owned a significant portion of the Mexican oil industry and their investments were expanding. These interests made the stability of the Mexican government a matter of concern for the Taft Administration.[19]

The Mexican revolution suffered an early setback in 1911 when Francisco Madero, an insurgent leader, escaped across the

---

[18] Richardson, XV, 6973-7023 for Roosevelt's Fifth Annual Message of 5 December 1905, especially 6997-6999; Bemis, 166. The interpretation is also borne out in P. Edward Haley, *Revolution and Intervention: The Diplomacy of Taft and Wilson with Mexico, 1910-1917* (Cambridge: MIT Press, 1970).

[19]"Trading on the country's untapped natural wealth, Diaz was able to attract vast amounts of foreign capital. During the three decades of his reign, American and European investors were granted immensely valuable concessions on Mexican soil. By 1912, the American investment exceeded one billion dollars, a sum almost equalling the total capital of native Mexicans. Standard Oil, United States Steel, the Anaconda Corporation, Mexican Petroleum, and the Hearst and Guggenheim interests accounted for some of the more extensive holdings. In the aggregate, American firms owned 75 per cent of all the mines in Mexico and over 50 per cent of the oil fields." Jack Sweetman, *The Landing at Veracruz 1914* (Annapolis: Naval Institute Press, 1968), 9.

border into Texas and found refuge in the neutral territory of the United States. Initially he denied any intention of setting afoot a new revolutionary force, but he found great sympathy for his cause in the borderlands by praising the United States for all the rights and freedoms Mexico lacked. Soon Madero did take a small force across the border. When the revolutionaries were driven back by Mexico's Federal Army, Madero was arrested by the Department of Justice for violation of U.S. neutrality laws.[20] Madero's support was widespread by then, and there were even allegations Standard Oil was financing his adventures because Diaz was giving preferential treatment to British oil investors. In any case, the charges against Madero were quietly dropped. This failure of enforcement and Madero's growing moral and material support in the United States prompted Diaz to send the noted Mexican lawyer Joaquin Casasus as a special emissary, first to Texas and later to Washington to plead for enforcement of strict neutrality along the border.[21]

President Taft was wedded to the idea of providing protection to U.S. citizens and their property, but he was equally committed to avoiding the use of force without the express authorization of the Congress. Seeking a course to avoid confrontation and enforce neutrality simultaneously proved quite a challenge.

In March 1911, President Taft sent between 15,000 and 20,000 troops to patrol the Texas border and mobilized Army and Navy Units at Galveston, San Antonio, and Los Angeles. These actions, aimed at contributing to stability, missed the mark completely because the President neglected to notify Mexico of the purpose of these actions before they were taken. When Mexicans learned U.S. warships were en route to Mexican coastal states there was a great fear of invasion. Only after the First Secretary of the Mexican Embassy in Washington submitted a formal request for clarification did Mexico understand the

---

[20]Karl M. Schmitt, *Mexico & the United States, 1821-1973: Conflict and Coexistence* (New York: John Wiley & Sons, Inc., 1974), 112-113.

[21]Ibid., 115.

purpose of the force movements; tensions then quickly subsided. Recognizing the effects of his well-meaning actions, President Taft offered assurances of his intentions and ordered the ships to stop only briefly to take on coal and put back out to sea.[22]

According to one detailed history, the demonstration of force was not only poorly coordinated with diplomatic efforts, it came too late. This second time he launched a revolution from U.S. soil, Madero proved unstoppable. By the time the border patrols were in place, Madero already was established inside Mexico and soon seized the reins of power. Taft recognized Madero's government and pledged himself not to permit another counterrevolutionary force to stage from the United States and in fact established strict controls to prevent any factional force access to U.S. arms and munitions. The United States again mobilized troops along the border during the brief rebellion led by Pascual Orozco. This mobilization to control the border again gave rise in Mexico to rumors of impending intervention.[23]

On 2 March 1912, President Taft delivered a proclamation

---

[22]The Mexican government, ever conscious of the U.S. conquest of northern Mexico sixty years earlier, was likely concerned that the United States would exploit the internal upheaval for additional territorial gains. Magdalena Bay, on the Pacific Coast of Baja California, was considered a strategically important harbor and there were rumors the Japanese wanted to obtain a base there. The Kaiser had tried to buy the bay for Germany in 1902. This prompted the U.S. Ambassador to the Court of St. James, Joseph Choate, to write telling Secretary of State Hay "We have a decidedly exposed flank ... and the Germans are after it." quoted in Page Smith, *America Enters the World: A People's History of the Progressive Era and World War I* (New York: McGraw-Hill, 1985), 427. (Smith does not cite his source and this quote does not appear to be repeated in the official U.S. diplomatic documents published for that time frame). The Germans were greatly concerned about the situation in Mexico and at one point were supportive of U.S. efforts to resolve Mexico's problems peaceably. By 1914, however, the opportunity to have the United States distracted by trouble in Mexico became attractive to the Germans. U.S. warships headed for the Pacific coast of Mexico must have seemed threatening to the Mexicans indeed. See Schmitt, 113, 115-116.

[23]Schmitt, 115, 121.

warning the nation that U.S. neutrality laws would be enforced and private citizens should not meddle in Mexico's affairs. By September, however, Taft's concern for Mexico's internal situation and the potential for the Madero regime to enact laws inimical to U.S. interests caused him to issue a warning, tantamount to an ultimatum, to Mexico not to tamper with U.S. interests. When Madero's regime experienced its own stability problems the following month, Taft sent the cruisers *DES MOINES* and *TACOMA* to Veracruz and Tampico, respectively, to protect U.S. citizens. Madero prevailed, and when stability returned the ships were withdrawn.[24]

In February 1913, U.S. Ambassador Henry Lane Wilson sounded the alarm from Mexico City telling Secretary of State Knox "Our Government . . . should take prompt and effective action."[25] This time the threat to the Madero regime was real. President Taft responded to his ambassador's warning in time and six ships were put in place to protect U.S. citizens when the regime fell: *SOUTH DAKOTA* was sent to Acapulco; *COLORADO* to alternate between Mazatlan and Manzanillo; and *VERMONT, NEBRASKA, GEORGIA* and *VIRGINIA* to the Veracruz-Tampico area. It is noteworthy that the earlier naval

---

[24]U.S. Department of State, *Foreign Relations of the United States (FRUS)* (Washington, DC: GPO, 1870-), (1912), 732-733 and Haley, 31, 39, 42, 44, 51. J. R. Clark, Jr., Solicitor for the Department of State, from "The Mexican Situation", 1 October 1912, in Philander C. Knox Papers, Library of Congress, Accession 3686, Bound Pamphlets, Correspondence 19:3110, quoted in Haley, 49. Shortly thereafter (March 14th), an expansive neutrality law was passed aimed more at establishing a domestic policy to keep the United States out of Mexico's war than to implement any obligations of international law (*USStat* 37, 630, which forbid U.S. citizens, or anyone else, from supporting either side from U.S. soil. It is included in the collection of neutrality legislation and treaties for the United States in Francis Deák and Philip C. Jessup, eds., *A Collection of Neutrality Laws, Regulations, and Treaties of Various Countries* [Washington: Carnegie Endowment for Peace, 1939], 1089). See also note 27 infra.

[25]*FRUS* (1913), 700, file no. 812.00/6058, telegram of 10 February 1913 from U.S. Ambassador Wilson to Secretary of State Knox.

demonstration was conducted with two small cruisers and this one involved two large cruisers and four battleships, a significant escalation, both quantitatively and qualitatively that must have been recognized by the Mexicans. The ships' mission was to protect U.S. citizens and foster stability, but once these large cruisers and battleships were on station, Ambassador Wilson took it upon himself to call upon Madero and threaten to intervene unless foreign interests were protected and the fighting stopped. Madero agreed and wired Taft pleading for restraint and offering to compensate all U.S. citizens' losses. Despite his personal philosophy regarding intervention, Taft was not going to be caught unprepared. He embarked 2,000 Marines in transports at Guantanamo, and an additional 5,000 soldiers embarked at Galveston before the *Decena Tragica* was over.[26] Madero's regime fell to the forces of General Victoriano Huerta.

An investigation led to the dismissal of Ambassador Wilson for his personal intervention with Madero (done in the name of the United States), but Taft and Knox, perhaps unwittingly, had also played key roles in the undermining of Madero's position. Their indiscriminate flexing of armed force helped weaken two successive Mexican governments while the stated Administration goal was only to protect U.S. citizens, property, and economic interests and preserve stability.

President Wilson Confronts Huerta

Instability in Mexico continued as Woodrow Wilson came to office in March 1913. In Wilson's view, the ascendance of the perfidious General Huerta was worse than instability. Wilson considered Huerta wholly unworthy of ruling Mexico because he

---

[26]Haley, 64-65, 66-68 and 68-69; Schmitt, 123. There had been rumors of Victoriano Huerta, a general under Madero and perpetrator of this revolt, attempting a coup as early as September 1912, see *FRUS* (1912), 841, file no. 812.00/4933, the U.S. Consul at Nuevo Laredo (Garrett) to Secretary of State Knox, telegram, 15 September 1912. *Decena Tragica* refers to the "Ten Tragic Days" of the Mexican Revolution, 9-18 February 1913.

believed that government always should enjoy the consent of the governed. Determined that his administration would not look with favor upon those who seized power, Wilson adopted a "legitimacy doctrine" making morality a priority in U.S. foreign policy, and Huerta did not pass Wilson's moral litmus test for legitimacy. Consequently, he felt obliged to make his legitimacy policy effective by sending John Lind as a special envoy to Mexico to promote the idea of elections (which would not include Huerta as a candidate). Huerta was confident the United States would not intervene unless the President could expect overwhelming public support for such action, and there was no such support.[27]

Huerta, however, could not be so sanguine about events inside Mexico. An insurrection under Venustiano Carranza, a leader in the Constitutionalist faction, was gathering momentum, and in his quest to consolidate power Huerta apparently allowed his police to kill Mexican Senator Belisario Domingues. This led President Wilson to abandon private diplomacy. The United States called on other nations to join in trying to persuade Huerta

---

[27]Arthur S. Link, *Woodrow Wilson and the Progressive Era: 1910-1917* (New York: Harper & Brothers, 1954), 107-114; Schmitt, 127, 131-132; Samuel Eliot Morison and Henry Steele Commager, *The Growth of the American Republic*, 2v. (New York: Oxford University Press, 1954), II:440-441; and John Lind to Secretary of State Bryan, 18 August 1913, the Papers of Woodrow Wilson, Library of Congress, Ser. 2 quoted in Haley, 99. See Richardson, XVI, 7884-7888, especially 7885-7887, for the text of President Wilson's special message to Congress in which he explains John Lind's mission and Huerta's rejection of Lind and asserts: "It is now our duty to show what true neutrality will do to enable the people of Mexico to set their affairs in order again. . . . I deem it my duty to exercise the authority conferred upon me in the law of March 14, 1912, to see to it that neither side of the struggle . . . receive any assistance from this side of the border. I shall follow the best practice of nations in the matter of neutrality by forbidding the exportation of arms or munitions of war of any kind." Also in Commager, *Documents*, II:267-269, doc. 393. The law the President referred to is *USStat* 37, 630 which forbid U.S. citizens, or anyone else, from supporting either side from U.S. soil. It is included in Deák and Jessup at 1089.

to retire, but Wilson's more public diplomacy was ineffective. President Wilson then proved that Huerta had underestimated his personal commitment to the "legitimacy doctrine." The President decided to unseat Huerta using whatever level of force might be necessary and instructed naval forces in the area to be prepared to assist U.S. and third country nationals should force be necessary. The months following saw impartial neutrality discarded as relations grew openly closer with, and supportive of, Carranza's Constitutionalist faction.

Carranza's representative in Washington, Luis Cabrera, was successful in first obtaining covert arms shipments, despite the U.S. embargo Taft had established, and ultimately in having the embargo lifted altogether. Given the state of relations at the time, lifting the embargo directly benefitted Carranza at Huerta's expense. Wilson told the Congress and the people of the United States that this action was intended to bring U.S. policy into line with the "law of neutrality." (Remember, the embargo was imposed to comply with neutrality as well). While lifting the embargo theoretically may have been consistent with neutrality, the motivation in doing it was clearly partial to the Constitutionalist cause. Wilson's intention was to let the Constitutionalists get rid of Huerta for Mexico.[28]

---

[28]*FRUS* (1913), 836-841 and especially 837, file no. 812.00/9178a, 12 October 1913, telegram, Secretary of State Bryan to the U.S. *Charge d' Affaires* (O'Shaughnessy) which instructs O'Shaughnessy to tell the Mexican Foreign Minister, "The United States . . . could not be indifferent to the political execution of officials." See also Haley, 106-107, and Link, *Woodrow Wilson and the Progressive Era: 1910-1917*, 117-119. Also Secretary of State Bryan to the U.S. Ambassador to the Court of St. James (Page), 19 November 1913, U.S. National Archives, General Records of the Department of State, Record Group 59, Internal Affairs of Mexico, 1910-1929, 812.00/9817a quoted in Haley, 123, states, "The President feels it is his duty to force Huerta's retirement, peacefully if possible but forcibly if necessary. . . . or, if not, that Constitutionalists (under Carranza) can compel his retirement without necessity for employment of force by us." Further, in response to British concerns for foreign lives and property in Mexico (which the United States claimed responsibility for under the Monroe Doctrine) President Wilson wrote, "The

Early in 1914 a naval demonstration was conducted off both Mexican coasts. While no blockade was attempted it was quite clear U.S. power could be brought to bear quickly. U.S. forces operating in support of U.S. policy again entered the territorial waters of a state whose policies the naval forces were trying to influence during a civil war and problems resulted which dangerously increased tensions.

The infamous "Tampico Incident" of 9 April 1914 precipitated (or according to some, provided the excuse for) the occupation of Veracruz. One of the ships in the inner harbor at Tampico, *U.S.S. DOLPHIN*, sent a party ashore in a small boat to buy gasoline for the Admiral's barge. Two Federal Mexican Gunboats in the harbor were shelling Constitutionalist forces just outside the city by firing over Tampico and were supposed to establish a blockade of Tampico, but Admiral Frank F. Fletcher, Commander of U.S. Naval Forces off the east coast of Mexico, had told them the city would remain open. The sailors were so unconcerned, however, that no one in the boat was even armed. Upon arrival at a pier, the sailors were arrested by members of Huerta's army. Two were taken from *DOLPHIN's* whaleboat, which was operating under the U.S. flag, and thus the boat's "territorial integrity" was violated by the arrest.[29]

Rear Admiral Henry T. Mayo, Commander Fourth Division U.S. Atlantic Fleet was embarked in *DOLPHIN* because the battleships could not cross the bar. He received the report of the arrests about the time the sailors were released. His immediate

---

United States government intends . . . to exert every influence it can exert to secure Mexico a better government under which all business and contracts and concessions will be safer than they have been. . . . We have also instructed our naval commanders on the coasts to render every possible assistance not only to our own citizens but to the nationals of other countries." Woodrow Wilson to Sir William Tyrell (private secretary to the British Foreign Minister), 22 November 1913, Wilson Papers, Ser. 3, 7:234 quoted in Haley, 121-122. *FRUS* (1914), 447-448; Schmitt, 136; Haley, 128; and George Harvey, "The Tragedy of Mexico", 202 *North American Review* (1915), 322.

[29]Sweetman, 30-33.

response was to insist Mexico apologize and fire a salute to the flag of the United States. Huerta apologized but would fire the salute only if Mayo assured him it would be answered in kind. Mayo accepted no conditions. The President wanted to back up Mayo's demand (issued without coordination with Washington). On 20 April, President Wilson asked Congress for approval to use the armed forces of the United States as necessary to obtain from Huerta recognition of the "rights" of the United States.

The President, as Commander-in-Chief, already had the authority and the obligation to use the armed forces to protect U.S. rights already. In asking Congress for their cooperation and approval to use force as necessary, Wilson foreshadowed the war powers debate that ensued decades later. Wilson must have seen this as a task that exceeded his direct responsibilities regarding defense of U.S. rights (especially in the case of our "rights" regarding a salute to the flag). In essence, the President sought Congressional authority to go to war with Huerta under international law without appearing to do so in the eyes of the U.S. Constitution.

The Senate resolution, which passed *after* the landing at Veracruz, called the President's action "justified" rather than "authorized" to stress they did not consider the resolution a declaration of war.[30]

According to a variety of contemporary accounts and well researched historical reports, sailors and Marines landed at Veracruz on 22 April 1914. While the stated motivation for the operation was to obtain a salute to the U.S. flag, after Veracruz was seized the salute was apparently never demanded.[31]

Additional insight to the President's (but not Admiral Mayo's) motivation is gained when it is understood the steamship

---

[30]Richardson, XVII, 7934-7935 also in Commager, II:271-272, doc. 395; *FRUS* (1914), 448-493 especially 474-475; Schmitt, 136-137 and Haley, 131-133.

[31]See Sweetman (note 19 supra) for an exceptionally detailed and stirring account of the situation and the action which saw 55 sailors and Marines awarded the Medal of Honor.

YPIRANGA of the German-American Line was expected to moor at Veracruz 4 hours after the landing began. *YPIRANGA* was carrying 200 machine guns and 15 million rounds of ammunition the Constitutionalists wanted to keep out of the hands of Huerta's forces. Because the United States was not prepared to go to war, the naval forces present were not conducting a blockade and the cargo could be considered contraband only by the Constitutionalists. The United States occupied the customs house at Veracruz, but *YPIRANGA* landed her cargo and delivered it to Huerta's forces at Puerta Mexico, too late to help Huerta.

The most pressing objective of the U.S. operation had ultimately failed:[32] the salute was not fired, U.S. citizens and their property were still at risk in Mexico, and the *YPIRANGA* 's guns and ammunition delivered. All the United States came away with was 13 dead sailors and 4 dead Marines.[33] The operation did

---

[32]Jack Sweetman provides a detailed account of a late night four way phone call to the White House. The U.S. Consul in Veracruz, William W. Canada, reported to Secretary of State Bryan that *YPIRANGA* would soon land the arms. Bryan called Secretary of the Navy Josephus Daniels and together, at 2AM, they called the President's Secretary, Joseph Tumulty, who apparently slept at the White House. They woke the President who decided that preventing the ship's arrival was important enough to act immediately. This is significant because the approval of the Senate, which the President had worked so hard for, and was not yet obtained—but could have been in just a few hours. See Sweetman, 47-49. It is unclear why *YPIRANGA* chose Puerto Mexico to land its cargo.

[33]*FRUS* (1914), 509-510, file no. 812.00/23445, Secretary of State Bryan to the Special (ABC) Commissioners, 27 May 1914, (drafted on Wilson's personal typewriter and carrying revisions in his hand writing); Wilson Papers, Ser. 2 quoted in Haley, 146 reveal this pledge and policy assessment: "We will not make war on the Mexican people to force upon them a plan of our own based upon a futile effort to give a defeated party equality with a victorious party. . . . A plan which would require the backing of force would if acted on do Mexico more harm than good and would postpone peace indefinitely, not secure it." See also Haley, 145, 150; *FRUS* (1914), 620-622; Hill, 556; and Sweetman, Appendices 3 and 4, 182-185. The complexity of developing useful U.S. policy for internecine civil wars appears to have progressed little over the last eight decades.

establish the partiality of the United States—while not being able to claim a causal relationship to the change of government in Mexico in the summer of 1914, the occupation of Veracruz certainly contributed to Carranza's victory.[34] The President limited his objective to the removal of Huerta from power and publicly renounced any effort to dictate the form of a new Mexican government, emphasizing this promise by removing U.S. forces from Veracruz in November even though Carranza's Constitutionalists themselves became factionalized—but domestic critics who frowned upon the initial landing were no more pleased with the withdrawal. After Huerta lost, Veracruz was formally delivered to Carranza and Villa in November 1914 after 6 month's occupation by U.S. troops, without any guarantee regarding the safety of American citizens.

By mid-1915 Wilson was totally frustrated with the situation in Mexico and issued a statement calling on factional leaders to end the strife and suffering in Mexico before the United States did it for them. When this ultimatum had no effect on the situation Wilson again overtly took sides granting Carranza's regime recognition as the *de facto* government.[35] The enormous share of its economy controlled by U.S. interests made Mexico's internal war a domestic political concern for the United States and impartiality regarding the contending belligerent forces impossible. Wilson also prohibited the export of arms to Mexico yet another time but allowed deliveries to continue to the Carranza regime. Even if Wilson's earlier reversal of Taft's embargo was due to differing interpretations of the law of neutrality, there is no rationale to interpret Wilson's Administration as complying with neutral duties after being on

---

[34]Haley, 133-134; Schmitt, 138-138n; Harvey, 323; David Jayne Hill, "President Wilson's Administration of Foreign Affairs—II", 204 *North American Review* (1916), 555; see also John Arthur Garraty, *Henry Cabot Lodge: A Biography* (New York: Alfred A. Knopf, 1953), 301-305 and William Manchester, *American Caesar: Douglas MacArthur, 1880-1964* (Boston: Little, Brown & Co., 1978), 73-76.

[35] Richardson, XVII, 8090-8091, Executive Order of 19 October 1915.

both sides of this issue.[36] Wilson was apparently convinced that the best course for the United States was to support the Carranza government and hope it would eventually be in a strong enough position to guarantee the rights of all foreigners.

AVOIDING WORLD WAR I

In sum, the second decade of the 20th century saw the United States struggle with the responsibilities which foreign investments bring. A pattern of behavior was emerging. Commitment to neutrality notwithstanding, the United States interests were forcing involvement where they never had before.

August 1914 probably marks the zenith of impartiality in U.S. foreign relations in the 20th century. War engulfed Europe, but Washington was determined to stay clear of it. On 20 August 1914, President Wilson told the people of the United States to be "impartial in thought as well as action,"[37] leaving

---

[36]*FRUS* (1915), 694-695 recounts the President's Statement of 2 June 1915 which warned: "If they cannot accommodate their differences and unite . . . this government will be constrained to decide what means should be employed by the United States in order to help Mexico save herself and serve her people." See also Haley, 163. There may have been moral, if not legal, grounds to take such "humanitarian" action. For example, Piedras Negras in early 1916 reported starvation conditions and food riots. Both Mexico City and Veracruz in the same year saw unsuccessful government attempts to fix food prices and force hoarded cereals onto the public market. In late 1916, it was reported that the mass of the poor—always a majority—suffered from starvation and lack of clothing, with an average of about a hundred dying every day. C. C. Cumberland, *Mexico & the Struggle for Modernity* (New York: Oxford University Press, 1968), 247-248; *FRUS* (1915), 771, file no. 812.00/165326, Secretary of State Lansing to the confidential agent of the *de facto* Government of Mexico (Arredondo), 19 October 1915; and Haley, 182. The arms embargo was imposed by a Presidential Proclamation of 19 October 1915, Richardson, XVII, 8089-8090. International law on humanitarian intervention remains controversial today though.

[37]"An Appeal by the President of the United States to the Citizens of the Republic, Requesting Their Assistance in Maintaining a State of Neutrality During the European War", Richardson, XVII, 7978-7979, quote at 7979; also

little doubt about the chief executive's awareness that even public statements by government officials could ill afford to be seen as biased in favor of any belligerent if U.S. neutrality was to be preserved.

The Hague Conventions of 1899 and 1907 recognized the true global interest in averting war. They also established extensive rules designed to reduce the horror of war once it erupted and put into place neutrality regimes to inhibit the spread of war to other states. World War I was being fought, in large part, under the recently codified Hague rules. As such, neutrality was unquestionably understood in light of the impartiality that was the essence of the law codified at the Hague, but neutral states were having real problems when the rules were measured against the reality of war.[38]

Germany needed to prevent the resupply of Britain or suffer defeat; England found itself facing the same alternatives. The laws of war and neutrality were badly bloodied in the Atlantic.[39]

Submarine operations were unprecedented in maritime warfare and could not effectively conform to the established legal practice of warships acting as commerce raiders known as the "cruiser rules." Generally, these rules required merchant ships to

---

Fenwick, *Neutrality*, 108; and Commager, II:276-277, doc. 400.

[38]Regarding the Hague Conventions, see Leo Gross, "States as Organs of International Law and the Problem of Autointerpretation" in G. A. Lipsky, ed., Law and Politics in the World Community (Berkeley: University of California Press, 1953), 69. See Schindler and Toman, and George Grafton Wilson, ed., *ILS* III (1903), and George Grafton Wilson, ed., *ILS* VIII (1908) for the text of the Hague Conventions. Regarding submarine operations and naval battles, see Francis Whiting Halsey, *The Literary Digest History of the World War*, (New York & London: Funk & Wagnalls Company, 1919) vols. IX and X.

[39]Some argue that the United States entered World War I not in response to the symptoms of the problem (events) but because it considered its fundamental rights under the law of neutrality were being violated to an intolerable extent. See Francis A. Boyle, "The Law of the Sea", Remarks on the 75th Anniversary of the Second Hague Peace Conference,138, and Francis A. Boyle, "Summary Overview", 146, both in *Proceedings of the American Society of International Law* 76 (1982).

heave to when challenged and required that belligerents allow their crews to abandon ships, which would then be destroyed and to place their logs and important papers into the lifeboats before an attack commenced. Even this was not enough if the crews could not reasonably be expected to escape to safety. If a coast or other ships were not nearby, the ship needed to be taken as a prize or the crew had to be embarked in the warship that attacked their ship. Neutral ships were immune from attack if they fulfilled their neutral duties.

The vulnerability of submarines on the surface forced difficult decisions regarding their employment against merchant ships when they became indistinguishable from another controversial class of vessel—the armed merchant. The possibility that her prey might outgun her forced a submarine to treat all belligerent shipping alike and attack without warning. On the surface, submarines were vulnerable to gunfire. Using her torpedos on the surface would likely require her to maintain a steady course at close range while under fire; few captains would like their odds in that situation. It is difficult to say whether submarines or armed merchants did more to cause ships to be attacked in violation of the "cruiser rules."

In reality the armed merchant was a double-edged sword. This was not lost on the British Parliament, and in response to their negative reaction to the proposed policy of arming merchant ships, Winston Churchill, First Lord of the Admiralty, told Parliament on 10 June 1913:

> The House will perhaps allow me to take the opportunity of clearing up a misconception which appears to be prevalent. Merchant vessels carrying guns may belong to one or the other of two classes. The first class is that of armed merchant cruisers which on the outbreak of war would be commissioned under the White Ensign and would then be indistinguishable in nature and control from men-of-war. In this class belong the *MAURETANIA* and *LUSITANIA*. The second class consists of merchant vessels, which would (unless specifically taken up by the Admiralty for any purpose) remain merchant vessels in

war, without any change in status, but have been equipped by their owners, with Admiralty assistance, with a defensive armament in order to exercise their right of beating off attack.[40]

This argument apparently convinced Parliament. While there were two distinct classes of these vessels, in the eyes of the First Lord of the Admiralty, common sense, if not the law, made them all look the same through German periscopes. But the actions of submarine commanders were condemned in the court of world opinion—they denied neutrals their rights and were seen as barbaric. Whether she was armed or not the Germans had every reason to believe she was when *LUSITANIA* was sunk 7 May 1915, carrying over 100 U.S. citizens with her to the bottom. Public outrage in the United States was more persuasive than the niceties of any German legal argument.[41] Germany quickly abandoned its case when events in the Balkans led Italy to declare war on Austria-Hungary on 23 May. The fear of Bulgaria, Romania, and the Netherlands abandoning neutrality as well caused the Germans to heed the protest of the United States. A brief period saw Germany attempt to employ the cruiser rules,

---

[40]Winston Churchill (Parliamentary Debates, House of Commons, vol. 53 (1913), 1431) quoted in George Grafton Wilson, *ILS* XXVII (1927), 76.

[41]*LUSITANIA* had a brief but illustrious history of confusing the Germans and endangering Americans. On 6 February 1915 it is documented that her captain flew the U.S. flag to gain the benefit of U.S. neutral rights while crossing the Irish Sea en route Liverpool. After she was sunk with great loss of life and notoriety, Berlin issued a communique asserting that she was known to be armed and carrying contraband. See Halsey, IX:237, IX:255, IX:263-264. A variety of assessments after the fact dispute these claims, but it is reasonable to assume the Germans believed she was armed. They had gone to great ends to notify U.S. passengers not to sail in her and—at least initially—considered her sinking to be a great victory. The submarine's captain, Otto Steinbrink, had Germany's highest honor, an order *Pour le Merite* conferred upon him by the Kaiser. Halsey, IX:248-282.

but the armed merchants escaped most of the time.[42]

In early 1915, the British undertook to arm all their merchant ships since it was clear that submarines would save their torpedoes and attempt to attack apparently helpless merchants on the surface using boarding parties or with their deck guns. The results in terms of the survival of armed merchants attacked on the surface were remarkable even after the cruiser rules were

---

[42]See Richardson, XVII, 8062-8064, or Commager, II:282-285, doc. 405, for the 13 May 1915 U.S. diplomatic note regarding the *LUSITANIA*. The business of adverse opinion was not all aimed against Germany as Page reported to Wilson in a telegram dated 11 May 1915 regarding British public response to the sinking of *LUSITANIA*. "The respect and sympathetic silence of the first few days is now giving way to open criticism of American failure to realize the situation and of American unwillingness to act. There is a good deal of contempt in British feeling. This contempt is not based upon British wish for military help, but on the feeling that America falls short morally to condemn German methods and has fallen victim to German propaganda and does not properly rate German character as shown in war nor understand German danger to all free institutions. Fear grows of a moral failure on the part of the United States." from Burton J. Hendrick, *The Life and Letters of Walter H. Page* (Garden City, NY: Doubleday, Page & Co., 1925), III:242-243. See Richardson, XVII, 8127-8129 for German Foreign Secretary von Jagow's reply to the Protest regarding the attack on *SUSSEX* in which he asserts German submarines would follow visit and search procedures and "ordinary forms of cruiser warfare," 8128. See also Roger Dingman, *Power in the Pacific: The Origins of Naval Arms Limitation, 1914-1922* (Chicago: The University of Chicago Press, 1976), 35; Herwig, 117; and Halsey, IX:207-282. See *ILS* XVII 163-168 for the diplomatic correspondence bringing Italy into the war against Germany's allies in incremental steps until the last declaration, against Germany, in August. The attack on *SUSSEX*, referred to above involved a German submarine operating in disregard of the cruiser rules which torpedoed an unarmed English Channel Steamer. The ship broke in half at the bridge and two Americans were injured. Germany denied involvement in the attack initially but bits of phosphor-bronze from the torpedo were found inside the surviving part of the ship. Only Germany used phosphor-bronze in their torpedoes. Wilson issued an ultimatum that the United States would break diplomatic relations if international law were not observed. The Germans pledged to again follow the cruiser rules, apologized, and "punished" the submarine's captain. Halsey, IX:328-332.

again abandoned:[43]

> By April 1916 about 1,100 had been armed and results were quickly discernable: between January 1916 and January 1917, 68 percent of unarmed ships were destroyed by U-boat gunfire and only 22 percent escaped, while 3.9 percent of armed ships were sent to the bottom by gunfire and 76 percent escaped.[44]

This loss of effectiveness alone could have threatened the German efforts at lawful employment of their submarines and does not even consider the exceptionally severe risks involved in exposing the submarine to defensive fire from armed merchant ships carrying guns comparable in calibre to those carried by destroyers. Clearly, armed merchants enjoyed a significantly higher chance of survival against submarines if they were not attacked with torpedoes. The policy, legal, and tactical results of armed merchants cannot be accurately measured today, but much can be assumed considering the number of submarines now fitted with deck guns.

More important than the tactical questions posed by assuming all merchants were armed, however, was the strategic damage Germany suffered. The success of armed merchants improved the resupply of Great Britain, not to mention the extended consequences of contraband that reached the enemy. To make matters even more complicated for the Germans, the British

---

[43]"The British Admiralty had begun early in 1915 to arm merchant ships with two 4.7-inch guns because it calculated that German submarines carried relatively few torpedoes and hence nearly half of the time used their 8.8-centimeter deck guns to destroy their prey." Herwig, 121.

[44]"A number of small 'special service ships'—the so-called 'Q' ships—were also fitted with guns and designed to lure the unsuspecting submarine to the surface in order not to waste a precious torpedo on such small craft." Herwig, 121. See *FRUS* (1915) Supplement, 604-607, 849; also *FRUS* (1916) Supplement, 187-198, for correspondence regarding "Q-ships", armed merchants, and use of neutral flags by British ships. This correspondence includes classified British documents captured by the Germans which explained the weaponry installed in the ships.

blockade policy against Germany was so effective that merchant commerce in North Atlantic and European waters provided no benefits to Germany. The reciprocal benefits that usually make maritime law effective no longer existed.

The term blockade *policy* is used advisedly because the British, early on, had elevated the blockade above the scope of the terms "tactic" or even "strategy." Walter H. Page, Wilson's Ambassador to the Court of St. James advised President Wilson that his naval attaché had been told:

> To prevent Germany from receiving food or other help, (the British) might issue a proclamation that neutrals must not trade with Germany, and (the British) would be prepared, if necessary, to go to war with any neutral power, even the United States, that should disregard such a proclamation. In other words, in extreme need, they might practically forbid neutrality.[45]

Such an extreme would make no sense, but so extreme a statement wouldn't be communicated to the President by the Ambassador unless it couldn't be disregarded. Either the British were communicating desperation early, or they were trying to make a point to the attaché. No matter how it was intended (Page did state this was not the present British policy and obtained assurances to this effect from the Foreign Ministry), this communication from an ambassador posted in a belligerent state to his president takes on many of the characteristics of a British démarche. It could then be expected to have at least a subtle effect on Wilson's view of how U.S. neutrality should be shaped.[46] On the other hand:

---

[45]Letter from Page to Wilson dated 25 August 1914 in Hendrick, III:155.

[46]The United States later also protested British behavior regarding U.S. neutrality. See Richardson, XVII, 8143-8144 for the "Protest Against British Blacklisting of American Firms and Interference in American Trade with Neutrals" of 26 July 1916.

That the sinking of unarmed neutral ships was a clear violation of international law, Germany did not deny; but she justified her policy on the ground that it was necessitated by the equally lawless British blockade.

To Wilson and to most Americans the distinction between British and German violation of neutral rights was clear. As (Prime Minister, Lord) Asquith said, "Let the neutrals complain about our blockade and other measures taken as much as they may, the fact remains that no neutral national has ever lost his life as a result of it."[47]

The effectiveness of the British blockade denied Germany access to the same sources of war material regardless of a neutral's impartiality. In February of 1916, Grand Admiral Alfred von Tirpitz, then Secretary of the German Naval Office, wrote a memorandum for Theobald von Bethmann Hollweg, the German Chancellor, in which he reported U.S. financial interests in Great Britain were increasing and he predicted these interests would eventually bring the United States into the war. Consequently, Tirpitz depicted the United States as "a directly involved enemy of Germany."[48]

Although the United States was attempting to stop the war through diplomacy, it was also watering down its neutrality policy in favor of Great Britain as a result of domestic pro-Allied sentiments. The situation of Great Britain in the war and the violations of neutral rights at sea continued to worsen throughout 1916. While efforts could be undertaken to save the British from

---

[47]Morison and Commager, II:455. For an appreciation of how sweeping the provisions of the blockade had become see the "Order in Council Implementing measures to Prevent Commodities from Entering or Leaving Germany, 11 March 1915" from CIX *British and Foreign State Papers,* 217-219; also quoted in Joel H. Wiener, ed., *Great Britain and the Span of Empire, 1689-1971: A Documentary History* (London & New York: Chelsea House Publishers & McGraw Hill Book Co., 1972), 651-653.

[48]Der Weltkrieg No. 18 (secret), Tirpitz memorandum for Bethmann Hollweg dated 8 February 1916, Auswaertiges Amt, Bonn, Federal Republic of Germany (Foreign Office) quoted in Herwig, 119.

defeat, the sentiment was not yet strong enough to justify entering the war.[49]

> By the end of 1916 it was plain that (the U.S.) neutral status had again been made unsafe through the ever increasing aggression of the German autocracy . . . this conflict was the last *great* war in which (the United States) would remain neutral.[50] (emphasis added)

Germany's dilemma was, how much neutral trade with its enemy was too much? When did Germany benefit from accepting the risk of direct U.S. involvement because indirect involvement was too damaging to German interests? It is curious that the neutrality of the United States was not more broadly challenged by Germany. It would seem that the thought of the United States as a potential adversary was a greater threat than its bias toward the Allies.

Germany, however, was entering a do or die environment. According to Herwig's analysis, this was clearly reflected by Admiral Henning von Holtzendorf, the Chief of the Admiralty Staff, telling Field Marshal Paul von Hindenburg on 22 December 1916 that war with America was such a serious matter that everything must be done to avoid it. But he also felt that the submarine was the weapon that would bring victory to Germany, believing the United States would not be able to resupply

---

[49]"President's Special Message to the Congress of 19 April 1916 Regarding Submarine Warfare", Richardson, XVII, 8121-8124, in which Wilson stated his intention to "sever diplomatic relations."

[50]"How the War Came to America", Richardson, XVII, 8282-8299. Also, "Harassed by both belligerents President Wilson had come to the conclusion by October 16, 1916, that the 'business of neutrality' was over, and that no nation must henceforth be permitted to declare war and set in motion forces so destructive to the normal commerce of peaceful nations." Charles G. Fenwick, *International Law*, 3rd ed., (New York: Appleton-Century Crofts, 1948), 613.

For a succinct statement of just how much the view of law had changed in London within a few short years see Page's letter to Wilson dated 15 October 1914, in Hendrick, III:176-180.

Germany's enemies fast enough in the face of unrestricted submarine warfare. Further, he believed even if the United States joined the war openly, U.S. troops would have to run the gauntlet of German submarines before they could land in Europe and begin to make a difference. Holtzendorf argued for renewal of the unrestricted submarine warfare campaign, saying that there was no other choice, even if it brought the United States into the war. Hindenburg agreed on Christmas eve.[51]

By 1 February 1917 unrestricted submarine warfare had recommenced. History recorded the accuracy of Holtzendorf's assessment. The United States broke diplomatic relations with Germany 2 days later.[52]

In March, with the United States still legally at peace with Germany, U.S. armed merchants went to sea with orders to fire on hostile submarines.[53] In the same month Germany's submarines sent four still unarmed U.S. flag vessels to the bottom. On 2 April 1917, President Wilson asked Congress for a declaration of war. Congress obliged, and the President declared war on 6 April. A major force behind the U.S. decision to forsake neutrality and bring its military power to bear as a belligerent was the German policy of unrestricted submarine warfare against neutral merchant ships.[54]

---

[51]Herwig, 121-123.

[52]"Diplomatic Relations With Germany Severed" (An Address to the Joint Session of Congress on 3 February 1917 by President Wilson), Richardson, XVII, 8206-8209.

[53]See Richardson, XVII, 8209-8212 regarding the arming of U.S. merchant ships.

[54]Text of Joint Resolution declaring war at Richardson, XVII, 8299; see also George Grafton Wilson, ed., *ILS* XVII (1917,) 222-229; Bailey, 591-593; and Fenwick, 79. See Richardson, XVII, 8226-8233, and Commager, II:308-312, doc. 418 for the text of President Wilson's speech declaring war on Germany. The declaration was justified based on the following rationale: "I thought it would suffice to assert our neutral rights with arms. . . . But armed neutrality . . . is impracticable. Because submarines are in effect outlaws . . . it is impossible to defend ships against their attacks as the law of nations has assumed that merchantmen would defend themselves against privateers or

That unrestricted submarine warfare was precipitated by the arming of British merchant ships, U.S. trade with Britain, and the British blockade. This untenable situation brought about the termination of U.S. neutrality and, the United States could never again expect to sustain impartial neutrality where her interests were involved. In the words of Woodrow Wilson, "America . . . reached her (age of) majority as a world power."[55]

Even in the wake of the Hague Peace Conferences' codification of neutral impartiality as the best legal policy to inhibit the spread of war, impartiality for the United States eventually proved impractical and unattainable.

---

cruisers, visible craft giving chase upon the open sea. . . . They must be dealt with on sight, if dealt with at all. . . . Armed neutrality . . . is worse than ineffectual: it is likely only to produce what it is meant to prevent; it is practically certain to draw us into the war without either the rights or the effectiveness of belligerents." German influence in Mexico was also causing some consternation. See XVII Richardson 8295 regarding the "Zimmermann Telegram"; Haley, 248-259; and Halsey, IV:14-18.

[55]"Address to the Senate" (29 June 1919), Richardson, XVII, 8736.

3.
THE INTERWAR PERIOD

The world after 1918 tended to recognize a new jus ad bellum
*. . . and to distinguish . . . sanctions authorized by the League
of Nations from . . . aggression.*[1]

THE MORE THINGS CHANGE...

The turbulence of World War I was on the ebb, a war that
"spelled death to so many millions of men, spread desolation
over so much of the Continent of Europe and shocked and
imperiled neutral as well as belligerent nations."[2] World states,
individually and collectively, attempted at this time to restore the
international order and re-establish the force of the legal system.
World interdependence had grown; it was evident that war
anywhere might affect everyone. The "indivisibility of peace"
became an accepted truism.

In this environment the international community undertook
legal obligations that seem inconsequential today because, for the
most part, they proved ineffective in the face of determined
aggression. At the time, however, their intent and ethical
underpinnings were unprecedented.

Although the details of these efforts are beyond the scope of
this work, it is important to review at least briefly their influence
upon the world's view of neutrality's survival from World War
I and the rights and duties of neutrals.

---

[1]Wright, 192.
[2]Frank B. Kellogg, "The War Prevention Policy of the United States", *AJIL*
22 (1928), 253-261.

THE LEAGUE OF NATIONS

The League of Nations emerged as a direct result of the war. Its Covenant[3] was part of the Treaty of Peace. Agreement to the provisions of the Covenant was supposed to be part of legally ending the state of war. It asked too much, but it also promised a great deal:

> The era of legally unrestricted right to resort to war, neutral indifference to the aggressive use of force, rival alliances and competitive armaments, and cynical manipulation of power relationships was past. In the new era war anywhere would be everybody's business; discussion at the bar of world public opinion would supersede Machiavellian browbeating tactics; and the security of nations would be a matter of collective responsibility.[4]

The problems with the Covenant involved legal and policy matters perceived as going to the heart of a state's sovereignty. Some argued that Article 10 of the Covenant allowed the League to decide when member-states should go to war, in effect ending neutrality and a state's sovereign right to elect and conduct a neutral policy—at least as neutrality was framed in the Hague Conventions. The well-intentioned but unfortunate wording obligated members of the League to "preserve as against external aggression the territorial integrity and . . . political independence of all Members."[5]

Further, it was not easy to identify who decided, under the Covenant, when aggression occurred, determining which side was the aggressor was an obviously important decision if it bound states to act. Consequently, the threat that Article 10 might

---

[3]Article 10 of the Covenant of the League of Nations states, "The Members of the League undertake to respect and preserve as against external aggression the territorial integrity and existing political independence of all Members of the League. In case of any such aggression the Council shall advise upon the means by which this obligation shall be fulfilled." Text in Louis B. Sohn, ed., *Basic Documents of the United Nations* (Brooklyn: The Foundation Press,1968), 298.

[4]Claude, 55.

[5]Covenant of the League of Nations, Article 10.

require an unwanted and unnecessary war for the United States was one of the reasons the Senate refused its consent to the Treaty of Versailles and its included Covenant.[6]

The interpretation that neutrality essentially had been outlawed ignored the fact that this treaty provision did not claim to bind nonparties. Moreover, even with regard to parties, if they failed to act against external aggression despite the treaty's expectations, they could still choose neutrality. States bordering a war that chose neutrality could claim they contributed something by limiting the scope of the conflict. Certainly, weak states bordering a belligerent would not improve the situation by declaring war and sealing their own imminent defeat.

It seems remarkable, but for a variety of reasons—which were valid at least in part, and certainly proved exceptionally persuasive at the time—the United States stayed out of the League of Nations. President Wilson had crafted the Treaty of Versailles and the Covenant himself, but he was not the last president to find that the Congress of the United States is fully empowered to seek what it sees as the best course for the nation.

While the United States made a policy decision to stand alone, the world continued to evolve into a smaller and even more dangerous place. Industrialism and sea transport were bringing the community of nations closer together. While the United States viewed the oceans as defensive barriers, those same oceans formed its common border with all other maritime states, and thus they also became both the interior lines of communication of the United States and corridors through which the horrors of war could be delivered.

Article 11 of the Covenant made even the *threat* of war "a matter of concern for the whole League,"[7] but as later experience demonstrated, the Covenant, like the Hague Conventions and the

---

[6]See Richardson, XVIII, 8784-8795, and 8821-8823 for Wilson's rebuttal of Congressional Objections and related material. See also Garraty, chapter XX passim.

[7]Covenant of the League of Nations, Article 11 (1) codified the "indivisibility of peace" by stating, "Any war or threat of war, whether immediately affecting any Members of the League or not, is hereby declared a matter of concern to the whole League, and the League shall take any action deemed wise and effectual to safeguard the peace of nations."

Declaration of London, attempted to set out principles easy to believe in but difficult to apply. It would seem that some states felt they had accepted a commitment to refrain from war even when war might be in their national interest, but possibly to go to war when it was not, according to Professor Claude:

> The history of the League was a record of constant efforts to strengthen and to weaken the collective security provisions of the Covenant. This was not so much a contest between friends and enemies of the principle of collective security as a vacillation between the desire to enjoy the benefits and the urge to avoid paying the price of collective security. The League could neither take collective security nor leave it alone.[8]

The League's efforts might reflect an inherent flaw of all collective security arrangements, which are concluded for the purpose of dissuading other states from aggression. When these arrangements fail in their primary purpose of deterrence, too frequently only states directly affected are prepared to attempt to fulfill the arrangement's secondary purpose of re-establishing the *status quo ante*. Each time a state fails to undertake its responsibility regarding this secondary purpose it weakens the deterrent effect of any future collective security effort. Recent history in the Persian Gulf region proved that collective security can work if strong leadership, effective diplomacy, and a clear identification of the aggressor exist. The response to trouble in the Balkans, however, makes it obvious that consensus can still be elusive.

As for the Covenant's effect on the law of neutrality, however, claims that neutrality was forced into desuetude by the Covenant are inconsistent with the fact that some members of the League contemplated a return to neutrality, as a result of the League being consistently ineffective in both preventing and controlling aggressive war. Denmark, Finland, the Netherlands, Norway, Spain, Sweden, and Switzerland each considered withdrawal; their complaints were valid. Japan and Italy had

---

[8]Claude, 263.

both resorted to war in defiance of the League before the Soviet Union was expelled for invading Finland in November of 1939. By then, however, the League was in its death throes and cataclysm was again upon the world.[9]

THE HAVANA CONVENTION ON MARITIME NEUTRALITY

During the period when the League was still functioning, efforts to clarify the law of neutrality continued. If nothing else, these efforts confirmed that the international community did not believe neutrality had passed into history.

The Convention on Maritime Neutrality concluded in Havana in February of 1928 again espoused impartial neutrality as the only true neutrality. Since it was signed by the United States in the same year that war was renounced as an instrument of policy in the Kellogg-Briand Pact, it testifies to the U.S. interpretation that the impartiality requirements of neutrality were essentially unchanged (at least for the United States and the other parties) by events and treaties after 1907.[10]

THE KELLOGG-BRIAND PACT

Later in 1928, in an attempt to bring the power of the United States to bear, France proposed to conclude a bilateral treaty committing the United States to ensure French peace. Secretary of State Kellogg countered with an offer to join a multilateral treaty that would renounce war as an instrument of national policy. The result was the signing of the Kellogg-Briand Pact in August.[11]

---

[9]Wright, 210; Leo Gross, "On the Degradation of the Constitutional Environment of the United Nations," *AJIL* 77 (1983), 569.

[10]Malloy, IV, 4743-4750; Schindler and Toman, 865-872; George Grafton Wilson, *ILS* XXXV (1935), 119; Article 15 states, "acts of assistance coming from the neutral states . . . are contrary to neutrality." The Convention was ratified by the United States in 1932.

[11]See Malloy, IV, 5130-5133, for the text of the Pact of Paris (Kellogg-Briand Pact). Also cf. Kellogg, 253, and Philip C. Jessup, "The United States and Treaties for the Avoidance of War", International Conciliation, April 1928, 201. See also Robert H. Ferrell, *Peace in Their Time* (New Haven: Yale

Though the Kellogg-Briand Pact was developed in response to a French effort to draw the United States into an alliance, it certainly restored some of the moral force U.S. policy had lost when the Senate refused to consent to ratifying the Treaty of Versailles and the League Covenant. The Pact was a far cry from a legal equivalent of the Covenant, however. Some even believed the Pact established a justification for unneutral acts by aggrieved parties when the Pact was violated by another.[12] If this analysis is correct it would seem to permit the unneutral actions of the United States prior to the Japanese attack on Pearl Harbor, which brought the United States openly and completely into the war against the Axis. However, there does not seem to have been any appeal to the authority of the Pact to justify these actions.

AN ISOLATIONIST UNITED STATES

This reaffirmation of strict neutrality precepts was perhaps foreseeable, but the question of when states should be aware of a state of war existing, and when belligerency became a legal status, giving rise to rights and obligations, remained difficult to answer in the interwar period as force not called "war" was being employed on a scale identical with war.

The political and legal restraints on resorting to war in the decades after World War I were defined by the League Covenant and the Kellogg-Briand Pact. Declaring war would constitute an invitation to sanctions under the Covenant and could affect the options of neutral states to provide assistance to both the victim and the aggressor. Consequently, weaker states fell prey to aggression in the form of undeclared war. According to Hindmarsh, "Probably more casualties and a greater variety of military actions occurred in the course of the Japanese peace-time

---

University Press, 1952), passim.

[12]"A state signatory to the Briand-Kellogg's Pact is perfectly entitled to adopt an intermediate position between belligerency and neutrality if it holds that a state involved in hostilities has violated the provisions," Titus Komarnicki, "The Place of Neutrality in the Modern System of International Law," *Recueil des Cours* 80 (1952), I:482; also quoted at Whiteman, 11, 150; see also Hans Kelsen, *ILS* XLIX (1954), 165n.

invasion of Manchuria and Shanghai in 1931-1932 than many petty Balkan *de jure* wars."[13]

This was the legal and political environment President Roosevelt encountered in 1933. Perhaps his later prewar decisions were foretold in his inaugural address when he said, "If I read the temper of the people correctly, we now realize as we have never realized before our interdependence on each other; that we cannot merely take but must give as well. "[14] Options to "give" were politically limited because his administration took office during a period of strong domestic isolationist sentiment. This sentiment presumed an exceptionally favorable balance of power and a remarkable level of self-sufficiency, according to Manfred Jonas:

> The isolationism of the thirties . . . sought only to preserve the American government's absolute control over its foreign policy by avoiding any long-term political commitments, either actual or implied, to other nations. They advocated a form of unilateralism, a policy of independence in foreign relations which would leave the United States free at all times to act according to the dictates of national self-interest.[15]

More limitations were imposed by public opinion in the United States in the mid-thirties that ruled out the participation of the United States in another European war. The impact of the isolationists' attitudes and the support of the general populace for protracted neutrality probably had a byproduct antithetical to the objectives of the isolationists' philosophical approach. Other powers must have perceived that U.S. economic and military

---

[13]Albert E. Hindmarsh, *Force in Peace* (Cambridge: Harvard University Press, 1933), 92-93.

[14]Although F.D.R.'s official Public Papers have not yet been published a private set was begun during his presidency and at least the first six volumes (through 1936) were issued. These are no longer in print. The above quote was found in *The Public Papers and Addresses of Franklin D. Roosevelt,* compiled and collated by Samuel I. Rosenman (New York: Random House, 1938), II:14. See also Bemis, 258.

[15]Manfred Jonas, *Isolationism in America* (New York: Cornell University, 1964), 5; see also the comparison of the "belligerent" and "timid" isolationists' views of neutrality at 6-8.

strength would not be brought to bear in response to aggression they might contemplate. The deterrent effect of the possibility of unneutral or co-belligerent action by the United States was greatly diminished.[16] Not only did the isolationists ignore the effect of aggression on weaker states, they either failed to comprehend or resolved to endure the inevitable impact of that aggression on the United States as a result of its growing interdependence with the rest of the world.

The domestic political influence of the isolationists shaped the law of the land[17] to conform with their philosophy. In the view of Manfred Jonas, this was to no avail:

> In every existing conflict, and all those that could be foreseen, American neutrality legislation had the effect of aiding one side or the other. Since isolationists had tried to eliminate this dangerous contingency . . . their efforts to promote true neutrality through legislation must be considered a failure.[18]

The world was to become increasingly embroiled in situations challenging the wisdom of impartial neutrality and inviting the dangers of unneutral involvement deemed essential to national interests. This environment set the stage for the war it foreshadowed.

---

[16]Ibid., 1, and Fenwick, v-vi.

[17]See *USStat* 49, 1081; *USStat* 49, 1152; and *USStat* 50, 121 for the U.S. Neutrality Laws of 1935, 1936, and 1937, respectively.

[18]Jonas, 203.

4.
THE FRUITS OF ISOLATIONISM

The legal significance of "nonbelligerency" does not
permit of much doubt . . . the abandonment of a strict
impartiality demanded by the traditional law . . .
served to give rise to the belligerent right of reprisal.[1]

BACKING INTO WAR

The years immediately preceding World War II found the United
States in a state of national ambivalence. The horrible memories
of the great war had not diminished, and the isolationism those
memories nurtured expressed itself legislatively in the Neutrality
Acts of 1935, 1936, and 1937.[2] These laws were more restrictive
than international law required and their object was more than
neutrality. The Neutrality Acts were intended to keep the United
States clear of entanglements that might unwittingly lead to war.
In taking this more restrictive tack, "The Neutrality Acts . . . had
not abandoned international law, they had only determined not to
assert all possible rights under it."[3]

Valid concerns over the international situation as the world
slipped ever closer to war eventually replaced the dominant

---

[1]Tucker, 192.

[2]*USStat* 49, 1081; *USStat*, 49, 1152; *USStat* 50, 121.

[3]Bailey and Ryan, 34. Though Bailey and Ryan are not lawyers their
assertion is borne out in 11 Whiteman and my own inspection of the 1907
Hague Conventions. Professor Rubin points out, however, that international
obligations had almost nothing to do with the development of U.S. neutrality
laws. See "The Concept of Neutrality in International Law", 366, 371.

domestic desire for isolationism. When war swept through Europe in 1939, the pendulum of U.S. foreign policy was swinging from isolationism to internationalism with a force that soon proved irresistible. Domestic politics and public opinion combined to slow the United States' entry into the war as a belligerent but accommodated unneutral actions as a *de facto* "nonbelligerent."

The neutrality debate notwithstanding, in December 1939, the United States Maritime Commission issued orders to radio operators of U.S. flag ships to be circumspect in their discussion of the location of Allied shipping,[4] but back in October the President had authorized the reporting of any "submarine or suspicious surface ship" in "plain English" by the ships and aircraft of the U.S. Navy's neutrality patrol. They worked throughout the American Neutrality Zone established by the Declaration of Panama[5] to keep belligerent ships out of an area

---

[4]Pan American Union, Law and Treaty Series, No. 13, Decrees and Regulations on Neutrality, Supp. No. 1 (undated), 27 states, "The United States Maritime Commission, on 22 December 1939 issued the following notice to U.S. merchant ships and their owners: 'The Maritime Commission is in receipt of information (from the British Embassy) concerning an instance of a radio operator aboard a United States merchant vessel who was heard working another such vessel and at the conclusion of the sending, advised as to the destination of his ship and information as to a convoy of ships in the vicinity.

'The transmission of such information may have serious consequences as constituting unneutral service under various prize laws, and it is requested that the Masters and Radio Operators of vessels under your control be issued whatever instructions may be necessary to eliminate the occurrence of such incidents in the future'."

See also Whiteman, 10, 857. The neutrality patrol was established by the Declaration of Panama, the President's "in plain English" order was recorded in a manuscript in the U.S. Navy Department Library, Washington, D.C. entitled "Administrative History of the U.S. Atlantic Fleet", vol. I, part 1, 42; it is cited in Bailey and Ryan, 40-41.

[5]The Declaration announced the Act of Panama concluded among all of the states of the Western Hemisphere (members of the Pan American Union). See Samuel Eliot Morison, *History of the United States Naval Operations in World War II, vol. I* (Boston: Little, Brown & Co., 1984), 13-16. An extensive and detailed study of this period in our history, whose operations largely predated Morison's coverage of the war, has been provided by Patrick Abbazia, *Mr. Roosevelt's Navy: The Private War of the U.S. Atlantic Fleet, 1939-1942*

that reached up to 300 miles from the coastline of the Americas. Units on patrol were also required to maintain contact with these vessels as long as possible. The effect of this order was to alert nearby British merchant ships to the presence of this threat. Because the reports were in English, it also provided easy to use locating information, adequate for British warships to intercept and engage their enemy's ships and submarines. Further, while the United States avoided reporting Allied vessels, citing the danger of being considered unneutral under prize law, "submarines and suspicious ships" were reported and tracked in de facto cooperation with the British.

Secretary of State Cordell Hull asserted, "International law . . . does not recognize any intermediate status between neutrality and . . . belligerency."[6] That being the case, into which category did the Secretary place the United States? The implication is the administration was consciously and purposefully acting at variance from what it perceived the law to require. It could also be that there was a major disconnect between the Secretary and the President over which policy options should be considered appropriate.

In May 1940, when German victory on the Continent of Europe seemed almost certain, Prime Minister Churchill appealed to President Roosevelt, saying "You should proclaim non-belligerency, which would mean that you would help us with everything short of actually engaging armed forces."[7] While

---

(Annapolis: Naval Institute Press, 1975). See especially 61-132 for detail on the Neutrality Patrol. Other histories, monographs, and documents are noted infra. Especially useful for analyzing this period is Francis L. Loewenheim, Harold D. Langley, and Manfred Jonas, eds. *Roosevelt and Churchill: Their Wartime Correspondence* (New York: Saturday Review Press/E.P. Dutton & Co., Inc., 1975). With a brief commentary and informative footnotes added, it reproduces the texts of the two leaders private correspondence.

[6]*FRUS* (1940), I:753, in an aide-memoire sent by telegram from the Secretary of State (Hull) to the American Ambassador (to Argentina Armour); see also Whiteman, 11, 166.

[7]Winston S. Churchill, *The Second World War*, vol. II, Chartwell Ed. (Boston: Houghton Mifflin Co., 1983), 24-25; see also *FRUS* (1940), III:49n, Whiteman, 11, 166, and Bailey and Ryan, 82; "The term 'non-belligerent' was frequently used in 1939-1940 in a somewhat confused treaty situation, wherein arrangements of alliance do not necessarily bring a state into war that is being

"non-belligerency" had no legal definition, it certainly enjoyed a great deal of practice. Of course, practice without an intention to comply with the law is insufficient to produce law.

The United States never formally declared any departure from neutrality, but U.S. actions varied widely from the legal obligations of an impartial neutral. While never engaged at a level of intensity comparable to the combat ashore in Europe or Asia, the United States behaved in a clearly unneutral manner. In fact, long before the attack on Pearl Harbor, the U.S. Navy was essentially at war with Germany in the Atlantic. Because Germany could not afford to bring the United States fully into the war the U.S. transgressions were met with some restraint. So while asserting *de jure* neutrality, the United States exercised *de facto* belligerence, or better put—courtesy of Germany, *ex gratia* non-belligerence. Mr. Churchill's request was answered with definitive actions but lacked the nicety of a declaration (which would have been politically inexpedient for President Roosevelt).

Other statesmen were not so constrained in their treatment of the law in public pronouncements. After the fall of France on 17 June 1940, Italy, which had been "non-belligerent," entered the war, and Spain became a "non-belligerent," eschewing the impartiality of a neutral.[8]

The next January, Roosevelt acknowledged the fact the war was clearly the business of the United States in his State of the

---

fought by its ally.", Robert B. Wilson, "'Non-Belligerency' in Relation to the Terminology of Neutrality", *AJIL* 35 (1941), 121; see also 11 Whiteman 1965. The Prime Minister escalated the request to include the U.S. Navy convoying goods en route to British ports in an 8 December 1940 letter to President Roosevelt. He referred to the proposed action as a "decisive act of constructive nonbelligerency," Churchill, II, 563.

[8]Howard S. Levie, *The Status of Gibraltar* (Boulder, CO: Westview, 1983), 57; Stone, 405; "In July 1943 the British Ambassador in Spain presented to the Spanish Ministry of Foreign Affairs a memorandum dealing with instances of unneutral facilities granted or not denied to the Axis. This included complaints that Germans had been allowed to set up night observation stations on both sides of the Straits of Gibraltar in Spanish territory, to build up an espionage organization in Spain, to install radio transmission stations, and to set up meteorological stations in Spain." Sir Samuel Hoare, Viscount Templewood, *Ambassador on Special Mission* (1946), 197, 199-200, quoted at Whiteman, 11, 223.

Union address: "The future and the safety of our country and of our democracy are overwhelmingly involved in events far beyond our borders."[9]

In an attempt to shore up the British in March of 1941, the President provided 10 large Coast Guard Cutters and other military equipment to British forces through the Lend-Lease Act.[10] Those who believed the U.S. had forsaken neutrality were in agreement with Senator Taft who is quoted as saying the act actually granted Roosevelt power "to carry on a kind of undeclared war all over the world, in which America would do everything except actually put soldiers in the front-line trenches."[11] Prime Minister Churchill believed the Lend-Lease agreement and the cooperation between naval forces placed the United States very close to war with the Axis Powers. In his correspondence with Roosevelt he confided that the actions of the United States Navy might decide the outcome of the Battle of the Atlantic and that convoys were being routed to take full

---

[9]Franklin D. Roosevelt's State of the Union message of 6 January 1941, quoted at Whiteman, 5, 1000. See also Arthur M. Schlesinger, Jr. and Fred L. Israel, eds., *The State of the Union Messages of the Presidents* (New York: R. R. Bowker Company), III:2855-2861.

[10]"Act Further to Promote the Defense of the United States and for Other Purposes", 11 March 1941, 55 Stat. 31 (Lend Lease Act) the provisions of this act also permitted the repair of belligerent vessels in U.S. ports when considered in the interest of the defense of the United States. See also the exchange of notes concluded six months earlier on 2 September 1940 exchanging destroyers for the right to seek sights for bases at Executive Agreement Series 181, excerpted at Whiteman, 11, 252-253.

[11]Senate Debates , March 1, 1941, 87 Congressional Record, Part 2, 77th Cong., 1st Sess., 1588; see also Whiteman, 5, 1004 and Fenwick, 647. As an aside, it is worth noting here that the Lend-Lease Act did involve the United States all over the world. It is generally discussed in terms of support to the British but apparently the Act was also used to support the Chinese in their war with Japan. Significantly this support to an enemy of Japan was offered before the attack on Pearl Harbor according to Ronald H. Spector, *The American War with Japan: Eagle Against the Sun* (New York: The Free Press, 1985), 325. In the Pacific, U.S. military personnel were being released from their obligations to the United States to join the war on the side of the Chinese against Japan and a U.S. military mission was established in China to support General Chiang Kai-shek at Chungking.

advantage of its protection.[12]

The President was intent on walking a fine line. He was willing to be a source of wartime supply openly for Britain, but he did not want U.S. ports to become an operating base for a belligerent's forces. By the end of March 1941, however, the British were repairing their ships in U.S. ports.[13]

Attorney General, Robert H. Jackson, in a speech to the Inter-American Bar Association in Havana on 27 March 1941, attempted to explain away the U.S. actions stating:

> There has seldom, if ever, been a long period of time in the last three centuries when states, for their own self-defense or for other motives, have been completely impartial in relation to the belligerents. . . . It is safe to assert that the absolute category of neutrality on the one hand, and belligerency on the other hand, will not square with the test of actual state practice, there is a third category in which certain acts of

---

[12]Churchill, III, 146; "A neutral can disregard its duties as a non-participant if it considers its vital interests threatened—as the United States obviously did so feel in 1940-41. But in doing so the neutral forfeits the right to demand from the offended belligerent that behavior to which it would otherwise be entitled." Tucker, 198n.

[13]The repair of belligerent vessels authorized by the Lend Lease Act was perhaps a greater violation of neutral obligations than the exchange of bases for warships. See Wild, 6-7; Herwig, 227; Whiteman, 11, 279-280; *NWIP 10-2*, sect. 443e; and 1907 Hague XIII, "Convention Concerning the Rights and Duties of Neutral Powers in Naval War", Malloy, II, 2352-2366; Schindler and Toman, 855-864, Article 17 states, "In neutral ports and roadsteads war-ships may only carry out such repairs as are absolutely necessary to render them seaworthy, and may not add in any manner whatsoever to their fighting force. The local authorities of the neutral power shall decide what repairs are necessary, and these must be carried out with the least possible delay.", likewise the "Convention on Maritime Neutrality" signed at Havana in 1928, IV Malloy 4743-4750, Schindler and Toman, 865-872, Article 9 states, "Damaged belligerent ships shall not be permitted to make repairs in neutral ports beyond those that are essential to the continuance of the voyage and which in no degree constitute an increase in its military strength.

"Damages which are found to have been produced by the enemy's fire shall in no case be repaired.

"The neutral state shall ascertain the nature of the repairs to be made and will see that they are made as rapidly as possible."

partiality are legal even under the law of neutrality.[14]

At first blush it appears the Attorney General and the Secretary of State had a major difference of opinion about the requirements of international law. In retrospect, it is more likely the Attorney General's remarks were either apologetics regarding the actions of the United States or an attempt to expand, in this forum of potentially persuasive legal opinion, the U.S. interpretation of the aspects of the law that could justify U.S. actions that appeared to place the United States outside the parameters of neutrality. Although the major premise of his argument—that unneutral behavior routinely occurs—may have been true, it did not affect the way the world interpreted the requirements of neutrality.

The assertion that traditional neutrality was no longer complete was not mere political rhetoric justifying a sensitive policy (though it was that as well)—it was an assessment of the situation the world confronted in the years immediately prior to the United States' entry into the war. It became increasingly apparent that law was not restraining aggression, and neutrality was an ineffective policy for both powerful and weak states. The many states either fully embroiled in the war or painfully aware it might soon engulf them understood the assessment as incontrovertible fact:

> The violation by Germany of the neutrality of Norway, Holland, Belgium, and Luxemburg in the spring of 1940 had far reaching effects upon the neutral American States. Argentina proposed that an attitude of "non-belligerence" be adopted. . . . Uruguay proposed a joint declaration of the American Republics protesting the violation of neutrality in Europe, and this was adopted and published May 19, 1940.[15]

---

[14]Whiteman, 5, 1010; see also *AJIL* 35 (1941), 348. For a devastating rebuttal of Attorney General Jackson's legal argument see Edwin Borchard, "War, Neutrality and Non-Belligerency", *AJIL* 35 (1941), 618-625.

[15]Fenwick, 647. This demonstrates that the futility of neutrality as a protection against German aggression was understood outside of the United States. Aggression was seen to make a policy of neutrality useless to the neutral and beneficial to the aggressive belligerent. The position taken by

In the United States, however, public appreciation of this truth was slowed by strong isolationist sentiment.

THE PRICE OF VIOLENT PEACE

The naval officer, more than any other government official, is significantly affected by the political position of the nation in peacetime regarding armed conflict between other states. The well-worn maxim of serving "on the frontiers of freedom" has rung true with frightening regularity during this century. Today, very few really "Remember the *MAINE*" or even other ships lost "on the frontiers of freedom" during periods when U.S. policy (usually for good reasons) violated the principle of impartiality, in practice or in proclamation:

> Attacks on ships . . . played a major part in the outbreak in all but one of the major wars in which the United States has been involved in the last 80 years. These incidents were occasions rather than basic causes of war, but they are not to be overlooked because of that.[16]

Beyond those attacks that started wars, or more appropriately, rendered their admission to the opening ceremonies in blood, numerous Navy ships and planes have come under attack when war did not ensue. In the case of World War II some would contend that the first American blood of the war was shed in December 1937. The gunboat *PANAY* was anchored in the Yangtse River when Japanese aggression in China spilled onto her decks. A Japanese court of inquiry concluded the attack was deliberate. In fact, military commanders issued orders for the attack. According to historian William Manchester, "The likeliest

---

Argentina is especially surprising. Argentina had maintained a close relationship with Germany and had significant ethnic ties to Italy, another Axis power. Argentina did not overtly join the Allies until 1945 when the outcome of the war was predictable. This perhaps speaks even more strongly of the influence on world opinion of Germany's abuse of neutral rights.

[16]Ken Booth, "Foreign Policies at Risk: Some Problems of Managing Naval Power", *NWCR*, Summer 1976, 12.

explanation was that the attack was a test of American nerve."[17]

The "unneutral non-belligerence" of the United States began to have significant consequences for naval vessels in the Atlantic shortly after the signing of the Lend-Lease Act.

• On 10 April 1941 *U.S.S. NIBLACK* was conducting a reconnaissance of the approaches to Iceland when she encountered the survivors of a torpedoed Dutch freighter. As the men were being pulled from the water, *NIBLACK*'s echo sounder gained contact on what was believed to be a submarine closing for an attack. *NIBLACK* conducted a depth charge attack and the submarine appeared to retire from the action. The German submarine *U-52*'s logs, recovered after the war, report an attack south-southwest of Iceland that day, but did not report being attacked. Nonetheless, *NIBLACK* engaged what was believed to be a German submarine, and this is recorded as the first engagement of the war between the United States and Germany.[18]

• The historical case study of the last voyage of the *BISMARCK* by Ludovic Kennedy relates that it was a U.S. Navy pilot, flying a Royal Air Force Catalina, who located the German

---

[17]William Manchester, The Glory and the Dream, (Boston: Little, Brown & Co., 1973-1974), 1:210; Attache's Report from Tokyo, dated 22 December 1937 Ser. 325, *PANAY* Bombing, Issued by the Intelligence Division, Office of the Chief of Naval Operations, Navy Department, now held by the Naval War College Archives, Newport, Rhode Island; Payson Sibley Wild, Jr., *ILS* XXXVIII (1938), 129-150. The Japanese Government dissociated itself from the decisions of its military officers and quickly apologized for the attacks disciplining some of those involved. See Rear Admiral Joseph B. Icenhower, U.S. Navy (ret.), *The PANAY Incident, December 12, 1937: The Sinking of an American Gunboat Worsens U.S.-Japanese Relations* (New York: Franklin Watts, Inc., 1971) passim for a thorough analysis of the incident.

[18]Morison, I, 57 and 73. Jurgen Rohwer, *Axis Submarine Successes 1939-1945* (Annapolis: Naval Institute Press, 1983), 49. The submarine was commanded by Otto Salman. Rohwer's work was not available at the time Morison's was prepared. It includes material declassified later. Morison indicates that no submarine action was recorded there—but the lost ship and men in the water make clear the records were incomplete. The *U-52* attack was the only submarine action recorded in the North Atlantic that day. It is quite likely a match. The submarine may have been gone before *NIBLACK* attacked or may not have recorded it. I am indebted to the anonymous historian, who critiqued an earlier draft of this work at Naval War College, for calling my attention to this and other useful references.

Battleship in May of 1941, sealing her fate.[19]

• German records indicate that in June 1941 a U-boat launched an unsuccessful torpedo attack on the battleship *TEXAS*, believing she was a U.S. ship that had been given to Britain. *TEXAS* was unaware of the attack. (In fact the attack went unnoticed until German records were being reviewed after the war). The same month, America learned that the Germans had drawn first blood when *U-69* sent the U.S. merchant ship *ROBIN MOOR* to the bottom late in May.

• During the ensuing months, Commander-in Chief Atlantic Fleet Admiral Ernest J. King issued a variety of orders regarding actions in the Neutrality Zone. The general theme was that belligerent states' ships entering the zone should be assumed to be acting against the interests of the neutral nations of the Western Hemisphere. On 11 September, the *U.S.C.G.C. NORTHLAND* seized the Norwegian schooner *BUSKOE* off the coast of Greenland. *BUSKOE* had a Gestapo agent aboard, and the ship was sent to Boston.[20]

• In September another engagement was fought between *U-652* and the destroyer *GREER*. The official orders given to Atlantic Fleet destroyers were only to "trail and report," and thus the officers had no authority to attack. *GREER*, following those orders, held contact on her echo sounder for over 3½ hours before the submarine, believing she was under attack, fired a torpedo at *GREER*. The destroyer responded with depth charges, but the submarine was unhurt. Both sides had fired in self-defense, but now both sides knew that the shooting had started. Seven days later, on 11 September 1941, the President issued his famous "shoot on sight" orders to the Navy. Hitler would later cite the incident in his declaration of war.[21]

---

[19]Ludovic Kennedy, *Pursuit* (New York: Pinnacle Books, 1974), 145-146.

[20]Morison, I, 60-63 and Abbazia, 233-234.

[21]Morison, I, 73; Abbazia, 174, reports that the German commander of *U-203* knew he was firing at an American ship but disregarded his orders. He cites the German War Diary, *TEXAS'* log, Doenitz, and Farago. A decision to ignore orders seems a strange thing for a commander to enter in his official log—or to confess to Admiral Doenitz. Bailey and Ryan, 147-148, 170, 172-173, 241; Rohwer, 53, reports that *U-69* sank *ROBIN MOOR* on 21 May. "U.S. Ship Sunk in Atlantic, Reported Victim of U-Boat; Allies Nearing Damascus",

• "Hitler's special ambassador, Dr. Karl Ritter, visited the (German) naval staff on 1 October 1941 only to be informed that the admirals were "dissatisfied" with the Fuehrer's "overly cautious treatment of the United States." The Battle of the Atlantic was seriously impaired by Hitler's restrictions. The naval staff informed Ritter that Roosevelt would not declare war even if Germany torpedoed all shipping headed for the British Isles."[22]

• In October, the tanker *SALINAS* and the destroyers *KEARNY* and *REUBEN JAMES* were torpedoed. *REUBEN JAMES* sank with a loss of over 100 men. The United States

---

The New York Times, 10 June 1941, 1:1-7:3; "Submarine Attacks U.S. Destroyer *GREER*; Latter Undamaged, Drops Depth Charges; Leningrad Ringed, Say Nazis; Soviet Denies It", *The New York Times*, 5 September 1941, 1:7-4:4. (In this account the Germans denied knowledge of the attack, which was likely true at the time. Notably *GREER* had been recently recommissioned to meet the increasing demands of a war the United States was not fighting); Abbazia provides a stirring account of the action at 223-231; Churchill, III, 516; In his address delivered on September 11, 1941, the "shoot on sight" speech, prompted by the attack on *GREER*, President Roosevelt said: "In the waters which we deem necessary for our defense American naval vessels and American planes will no longer wait until Axis submarines lurking under the water, or Axis raiders on the surface of the sea, strike their deadly blow—first. Upon our naval and air patrol—now operating in large numbers over vast expanse of the Atlantic Ocean—falls the duty of maintaining the American policy of freedom of the seas—now. That means very simply and clearly, that our patrolling vessels and planes will protect all merchant ships—*not only American ships but ships of any flag*—engaged in commerce in our defensive waters. They will protect them from submarines, they will protect them from surface raiders.", Leland M. Goodrich, ed., *Documents on American Foreign Relations* (Boston: World Peace Foundation, 1942), IV:100 (emphasis added); see also Whiteman, 5, 993-997 and Kelsen, 166n-167n for the President's address; "From now on, if German or Italian vessels of war enter the waters the protection of which are necessary for American defense, they do so at their own peril." *Department of State Bulletin*, vol. V, no. 116, quoted in Payson Sibley Wild, Jr., *ILS* XL (1940), 18-24 and see 77 for the text of the German Declaration of War.

[22]Bundesarchiv-Militararchiv, Frieburg, West Germany (Federal Military Archive) PG 32046, Case 126, p. 478, entry for October 28, 1941 quoted in Herwig, 233.

was then, and remained thereafter, a *de jure* neutral.[23]   President Roosevelt was quite candid on "Navy and Total Defense Day", 27 October 1941, when he said in righteous indignation while the country claimed to be neutral:

> Very simply and very bluntly—we are pledged to pull our own oar in the destruction of Hitlerism . . . our ships have been sunk and our sailors have been killed.
> I say we do not propose to take this lying down.
>   Our determination not to take it lying down has been expressed in the orders to the American Navy to shoot on sight. Those orders stand.   The lines of our essential defense now cover all the seas. . . . Our Navy is ready for action. Indeed, units of the Atlantic patrol are in action.[24]

Actually, since the "in plain English" order of October 1939, they had been in action for over 2 years.

•   On 6 November 1941, *U.S.S. OMAHA* took the German blockade-runner *ODENWALD* as a prize off the coast of Brazil. After months of looking for German commerce raiders in the neutrality zone, *OMAHA* and *SOMERS* were en route to Recife for fuel when they encountered a darkened ship flying the American flag. Suspicious, the *OMAHA* sent a boarding party by boat.   *ODENWALD*'s crew attempted to scuttle her, but the damage from the scuttling attempt was controlled by men from *OMAHA*, and with a prize crew in control, she was escorted to San Juan.[25]

---

[23]"U.S. Destroyer Hit by Torpedos Off Iceland; Arming of U.S. Ships Voted by House, 259-138; Ships in Pacific Ordered to Safe Ports," *The New York Times,* 18 October 1941, 1ff; Bailey and Ryan, 197 and 205-206; see also Herwig, 231.

[24]"Franklin D. Roosevelt: Address on Navy and Total Defense Day Concerning the Attack upon the U.S. Destroyer *KEARNY*," October 27, 1941, *Department of State Bulletin,* V:342-343; Senate Document No. 188, 77th Cong., 2nd Sess., 120, text also quoted in Louis W. Holborn, ed., *War and Peace Aims of the United Nations: September 1, 1939—December 31, 1942* (Boston: World Peace Foundation, 1943), 55-56.

[25]Abbazia, 346-349. It is noteworthy that by flying the U.S. flag as a strategem of war ODENWALD's master had made it legal for *OMAHA*'s boarding party to come aboard. See also Janusz Piekalkiewicz, trans. by Peter

On 25 November 1941, while the United States still declared itself neutral, American forces landed in Surinam to protect Dutch bauxite mines. President Roosevelt had obtained permission from Queen Wilhemina of the Netherlands (then a belligerent) on the justification that "This country secures from the Bauxite mines in Surinam 2 million tons of ore annually or 65 percent of our total supply."[26] The reliance of the United States on external sources for strategic resources was clearly established by 1937. American dependence on external strategic supplies had been documented as justification for the use of armed force. Senator David I. Walsh argued the United States could not survive in the face of a powerful enemy for more than 2 years without reliable supply via ocean trade.[27]

American unneutral activity in the Atlantic continued unabated. The *Kriegsmarine* war diary entry for 6 December 1941 concluded that the fighting in the Atlantic made war with the United States a fact and only the declaration was lacking. Germany provided that declaration 2 days later.[28]

When the bombs fell on Pearl Harbor they did more than destroy ships and kill their crews—they dispelled the illusion of peace, disposed of virtually all remnants of traditional isolationism, and shattered the elaborate legal fiction of U.S. neutrality. As Manfred Jonas said, "The Pearl Harbor attack was not merely the beginning of a war. It was also the end of a bitter

Spurgeon, *Sea War: 1939-1945,* originally published as *Seekrieg: 1939-1945,* (London & New York: Tek Translation and International Print Ltd.), 172.

[26]Whiteman, 11, 458-459.

[27]William Appleman Williams, *The Tragedy of American Diplomacy*, 2nd revised and enlarged ed. (New York: Dell, 1972), 195. Although Williams is a secondary source his work provides some useful information which unfortunately is not footnoted for cross-referencing to the original. Senator Walsh certainly overstated U.S. vulnerability but his claim illustrated the growing awareness of the significance of the increasing interdependence to U.S. security.

[28]Bundesarchiv-Militararchiv, Frieberg, West Germany (Federal Military Archive) PG 32048, Case 128, 83-84, entry for December 6, 1941, quoted in Herwig, 234. Apparently, a hard copy of the War Diary now exists in English in the Naval War College Archives at RG8, series III. I also owe this information to the Naval War College reviewer.

political and ideological struggle."[29]   Robert Tucker summarized:

> In pursuing discriminatory measures against the Axis Powers in 1940-41 the United States departed from its duties as a neutral, and . . . furnished the Axis Powers with sufficient reason for claiming the right to resort to reprisals. But prior to its actual (declared) entrance into hostilities as an active participant the United States retained its status as a neutral.[30]

---

[29]Jonas, 2.
[30]Tucker, 197-198.

5.
ENTER THE UNITED NATIONS

The incompatibility between the demand for a new legal order and the defense of the old brought on the Second World War. And it is the same demand . . . that poisons the international atmosphere today and entails the risk of war.[1]

RECREATING THE WHEEL OF PEACE

Like its predecessor, World War II shocked the consciousness of mankind. The governments of the victorious nations had many conflicting objectives at the end of the war but they were able to find a least common denominator: the United Nations Charter. The Charter goes further than any document before to bring together the world's resources in the cause of peace. The United Nations has not been an unqualified success, but it has stood for some time as a mechanism for peaceful settlement of disputes and sometimes has found a route back to peace when disputes turn violent. The tool itself is worthwhile and should not be condemned for its lack of use during the Cold War. As Grotius explained:

> Right does not necessarily lose its nature from being in he hands of wicked men. The sea still continues as a channel of lawful intercourse, though sometimes navigated by pirates, and swords are still instruments of defence, though sometimes wielded by robbers or assassins.[2]

The United Nations is the world's attempt to improve upon

---

[1]Morganthau, 410.
[2]Grotius, Book II, chap. XXIV, para. VIII, 289.

the noble experiment begun by the League of Nations. The League had stronger mechanisms to ensure peace, but could not produce the consensus necessary to use those tools. The framers of the Charter did not reassert the broader authority of the Covenant in the hope that the tool would be used more often. Indeed, many provisions found objectionable to the United States when the Covenant was first considered (and later to League members who had initially accepted them) were changed in the drafting of the United Nations Charter to encourage the new organization to function where its precursor had faltered. Like the League, however, the United Nations was still to be the instrument by which the victors managed peace in the postwar world. Consequently, the Axis states and the "non-belligerent" Spanish were, at first, precluded from membership.[3]

One other major difference from the League should be noted. Both the executive and the legislative branches of the U.S. Government actively sought membership in the United Nations. Preserving international peace was seen as a prerequisite for a successful postwar world economy. Paradoxically, the realization that the United States had worldwide interests and responsibilities in the postwar period was coincident with reduction of the armed forces to little more than one-tenth of their wartime strength. Although this reduction was required by domestic political and economic imperatives its breadth and depth also represented an act of faith in the efficacy of the United Nations.[4]

The most notorious aspect of the Charter, in that it stood as a bar to effectiveness, is the much maligned veto power of the Permanent Members of the Security Council. The authority to wield the veto, combined with the politics of the Cold War, cast the United Nations into a somewhat different role than anticipated by its drafters. Determinations of aggression and decisions to confront it were frequently impossible to attain.

---

[3]Leo Gross, "The Charter of the United Nations and the Lodge Reservations," *AJIL* 41 (1947), 531-554 passim; Garraty, 379n-382n; Claude, 88.

[4]Wright, 136-137 and John Lewis Gaddis, *Strategies of Containment: A Critical Appraisal of Postwar American Security Policy* (New York: Oxford University Press, 1982), 23.

Since the end of the Cold War, consensus has been easier to come by. This has allowed the United Nations to take significant strides in the area of collective security. Unprecedented cooperation has put the organization back into unfinished growing pains, despite its five decades of experience. Only time will tell if the problems identified by "first time" operations will be afforded a chance to be solved by a "next time."

THE CHARTER

Neutrality

The provisions of the Charter of the United Nations regarding the use or threat of force by states bear directly on this discussion of U.S. neutrality.

Article 2 (3) requires the peaceful settlement of international disputes and Article 2 (4) proscribes the use or threat of force against the territorial integrity or political independence of any state. The Charter does not outlaw war. In fact, the provisions of Chapter VII make it clear the framers believed war would be necessary to confront aggression and make its victims whole again.

The commitments made by Member-States of the United Nations have not stopped the use of force. The wording of the Charter has only caused states to look elsewhere for a rationale to use force. At the same time, however, the wording clearly placed some actions outside the Charter. The practice of states over the nearly five decades since the Charter came into force clearly demonstrates that Article 2 (4) remains a rule "for" rather than a rule "of" the behavior of states. While this may be lamentable, it does not modify the legal effect of the proscription, only its political effectiveness.[5]

---

[5]Elihu Lauterpacht, *ASIL* (1968), 62; Jennings, 64; see also Alfred P. Rubin, "Misconceptions of Law and Misguided Policy", *NWCR*, November-December 1982, 61 suggests that Argentine violation of Article 2 (3), which requires states to settle international disputes by peaceful means, was the proper legal justification for the British counter-action in the Falklands-Malvinas conflict and Thomas M. Franck, "Dulce et Decorum Est," *AJIL* 77 (1983), 109-124, focusing on Article 2 (4) as applied to the same issue.,

Under Article 2 (5), member states may be called upon to demonstrate partiality in a dispute should the United Nations decide upon enforcement action under the provisions of the Charter. This requirement is inconsistent with the conception of neutrality expressed in the Hague and Havana Conventions, but this does not mean impartial neutrality is never appropriate.

To explain the legal relationship of Article 2 (5) and neutrality, an examination of the process for deciding upon enforcement actions and their likely implementation is required. Article 39 is the gateway to enforcement action. It charges the Security Council to determine if the peace has been threatened or breached and which of the contending parties to the dispute has violated its obligations under the Charter. Only when this has been agreed upon by a qualified majority can enforcement measures be taken.

These very provisions were cited by Switzerland as a basis for refusing to join the organization, arguing that they could require a compromise of Swiss neutrality. Neutrality within the United Nations was thought to be entering desuetude, based upon the principle *cessante ratione legis, cessat et ipsa lex*—the reason of the law ceasing, the law itself also ceases.[6] It seems clear that the reason for the law has not ceased.

Claims of outlawed neutrality take a stilted view of the Charter. While Article 2 (5) can be understood to require partiality, it must be considered in light of the entire text that clearly anticipates the possibility force will be threatened or used

---

[6]"At the first postwar meeting of the International Law Association in 1946, C. G. Dehn, a British jurist, took the view that 'the sovereign right of states to go to war' had gone, (and) that 'neutrality as a legitimate status had disappeared'." Whiteman, 11, 147; "War in the sense of equality of the belligerents and application of the law of neutrality equally to both, seems on principle to be outlawed." *ASIL* (1967), Quincy Wright, 56; "Article 39 . . . formed an . . . effective estopple to the use of classic concepts of neutrality since it centralized the peace-keeping functions in decisions of the Security Council, and thus made it virtually impossible for any member state to remain neutral while at the same time living up to its commitments under the Charter." Oglesby, 107; Elihu Lauterpacht, 208; A. Leroy Bennett, *International Organizations*, 2nd ed. (Englewood Cliffs, NJ: Prentice-Hall, Inc., 1980), 81; and *Black's Law Dictionary*, 207.

by states in contravention of the Charter. Article 2 (3) requires members to settle international disputes by peaceful means. Article 33 (2) envisages the Security Council calling upon parties to a dispute to undertake methods of peaceful settlement.

Should the Security Council achieve the consensus required to take forcible action or require partiality, it could also require impartial neutrality. If all states were members of the United Nations and had foregone their neutrality in compliance with an interpretation of Article 2 (5), there would be no states to provide impartial candidates or to serve as mediators or arbitrators to provide "good offices" for the parties to the dispute. (Even after enforcement action might be deemed appropriate, the resolution of a dispute will need to use the peaceful settlement procedures described in Article 33 (2)). While the Secretariat has sometimes fulfilled the role of objective third party, it would be difficult for the United Nations to take enforcement action and still be viewed as objective and impartial by the offending party.

Further, if enforcement action is taken through armed force against a state, it might still prove to be in the best interest of the organization for the Security Council to require some states to observe impartial neutrality. This could prevent the spread of fighting to the aggressor's weak neighbors that might otherwise be easily defeated and only worsen the task of those charged with the re-establishment of the *status quo ante*.

For example, during *Desert Storm* Jordan and Iran both claimed to be neutral. In fact, the problems in the region might have been much more difficult if both states had engaged Iraq or even been merely openly non-belligerent. Had Iraq crossed their borders during the 6 months of *Desert Shield*, political and tactical complications would have ensued. Combat operations might have had to begin before preparations were complete. Iran might have needed to be removed from the eastern regions of Iraq after the fighting ceased. King Hussein might have been unseated by Palestinians and their sympathizers in Jordan. As it was, as neutrals, both states could be expected to prevent the use of their territory by Iraqi forces. They would be obliged to hold any belligerent forces or equipment entering their jurisdiction, as Iran did with the Iraqi air force. Clearly, there were advantages to the belligerent forces operating under the aegis of the United

Nations of having the border states declare their neutrality.

Another consideration that might require neutrality within the Charter is the period during which armed conflict has already begun and the Security Council is deliberating what action it should take. During these periods, since the Charter bestows the authority and responsibility for determining whom to be partial for and against upon the Security Council, third states should remain impartial to avoid complicating the situation.[7]

Practice of states proved that while the law may have changed, the states that agreed to it had not. Throughout the Cold War it was impossible for all Permanent Members of the Security Council to agree on almost any issue in the context of Article 39, and and without such agreement it is impossible to meet the procedural prerequisites to take enforcement action—and therefore the partiality requirements of Article 2 (5) do not come into play either.

There are no guarantees that all future conflicts will find consensus in the Security Council just because the Cold War is over. Each of the Permanent Members still has national interests and it is improbable they will always align closely enough to provide consensus for an effective solution. When the Security Council fails to decide, each state is free to make this decision for itself. In that case, neutrality remains a valid option. Further, as Austria has argued, the behavior of the world in relation to great powers and the pattern that evolved regarding the veto in the Security Council allow neutral states within the organization to make a real contribution to peace.[8]

Self-Defense and War

One of the greatest dangers to peace is aggression under the political cloak of self-defense. The only legal route to the use of armed force on the initiative of individual states explicitly addressed by the Charter (in Article 51) is self-defense, and most military actions are justified as such. It permits states to assert

---

[7]Philip C. Jessup, *A Modern Law of Nations* (New York: Macmillan Co., 1948), 202-210; Whiteman, 11, 149; and Kelsen, 161.

[8]Alfred Verdross, "Austria's Permanent Neutrality and the United Nations Organization", *AJIL* 50 (1956), 67; see also Whiteman, 11, 157.

the right of self-defense in response to armed attack until the Security Council decides upon the appropriate course of action for restoring the peace and the *status quo ante.*

But all force used in response to an armed attack cannot be characterized as self-defense. Sometimes the action constitutes self-help—that is, exploiting the aggressor's breach of the peace to use force to obtain objectives not required for defense of territory and rights—that can be a violation of Article 2 (3), a gray area. States with different interests will interpret the same situation differently. While it is reasonably easy in theory to separate the two functions, the passions of armed conflict and the issues giving rise to it often cloud the distinctions in practice. Consequently, there is a tendency for fighting to escalate quickly in its earliest stages and for the distinctions between the participants to become legally complex for third states (including Security Council members) trying to assess what action should be taken. Even when states are closely agreed on their objectives at the onset of a conflict, they can easily depart company as the end of the conflict approaches.

Justice should not be sacrificed in the interest of peace. If it is, the quality and value of the peace will be damaged and further injustice encouraged. All nations' interests are indirectly threatened when injustice or aggression is not confronted with resolve, but before this can happen, a consensus is need that extends well beyond the Permanent Members of the Security Council.

Given that armed conflict can erupt and expand in the absence of definitive action under the Charter by the Security Council, questions of neutrality or partiality become matters of individual state policy; the Law of War and Neutrality must then apply. Less than impartial actions are going to be perceived by the belligerents as violations of the law of neutrality and, perhaps more importantly, as interference with attainment of objectives the contending belligerents already have assessed as important enough to justify spending the blood of their young.

Before deciding upon partiality, states must recognize that their actions will be evaluated by belligerents who will make their own policy decisions regarding those partial actions. The dangers inherent in this situation worsen the longer a rupture of the peace persists. The major problem the United Nations has faced regarding international security issues has been the inability of the Permanent Members of the Security Council to agree on the categorizations of most breaches of the peace.

In fact, when the Axis and their nonbelligerent sympathizer Spain were excluded, the Charter was originally intended to be a military alliance. It was expected to deter aggression by placing the power of its members behind the principles it enshrined. Those expectations were not always fulfilled. As Professor Gross noted, "The members of the League and the members of the United Nations now seem to be moved to moral indignation only in selected cases, which deprives indignation of its moral basis."[9]

The results of the League having followed this course are documented in blood, and although the ruptures have not been as cataclysmic, the U.N. experience is being written in the same hand. As long as violence continues as a policy option for states, neutrality will continue to play an important role:

> In the absence of any action by the Security Council or the General Assembly or if the resolutions adopted by those bodies are silent, the members remain bound by the old law of neutrality, including, as to parties thereto, the conventions adopted at the Hague in 1907.[10]

If Hague 1907 marks the state of the art in neutrality, impartiality is still the expectation. The neutrality regime concluded over eight decades ago still finds utility today, and, unfortunately, because war has not been effectively prevented, neutrality has not entered desuetude either.[11]

---

[9]Gross, "On the Degradation of the Constitutional Environment of the United Nations", 569.

[10]*ASIL* (1968), 73.

[11]"It is quite clear that once we leave the system of the Hague Conventions, the only codification of laws of neutrality, we begin to grope in the dark.", Titus Komarnicki, "The Place of Neutrality in the Modern System of International Law", *Recueil des Cours* 80 (1952) I:403. See also Whiteman, 11, 177.

EXPLOITATION AND ESCALATION

Faced with a Security Council that frequently has failed in the business of peacekeeping, the Secretariat has in many cases found itself assuming responsibilities for peacemaking. But in the sometimes protracted period between the Security Council arriving at a politically motivated impasse and the Secretariat, or some other entity, finding a route back to peace, there are important policy questions to be addressed by the United States.

How does the United States chart a course that is supportive of its national interests and will best foster peace in the global community? The emergence of international security organizations after both world wars was, in part, an attempt to bring the power of the United States to bear to maintain world order. No matter how she might otherwise be criticized, few would question that the United States continues to stand for freedom and democracy. This alone nominates her to champion the cause, but world peace and stability are also undoubtedly in the national interest of the United States, and it would be dangerous in today's world to leave them entirely to others. If some others filled the void, the absence of U.S. influence would likely work to the ultimate disadvantage of the United States and the world in general. Accepting this challenge, however, is equally dangerous. It will be essential to assess accurately those situations in which the challenge is also a responsibility because the price of accepting it is nonrefundable.

While the great powers avoid armed conflict with one another, smaller states are not always similarly restrained. Further, to prevent U.N. action to stop their use of force, these smaller states often seek the implicit backing of a great power in their efforts.

During the Cold War, this pattern of smaller states manipulating great powers had the effect of paralyzing the Security Council and frequently prevented other major powers from intervening militarily to stop them. These misadventures, however, can result in the direct involvement of a great power and pose an even more substantial threat to the peace.

Smaller states sometimes advocated the neutrality regime of the Hague Conventions to protect through law what they could not deter with their meager military power. Today great powers are well advised to observe the laws of neutrality closely unless a conscious policy decision is made to assume the risks of partiality. By doing so they will not be drawn unwittingly into hostilities taken by or against a client state.

6.
POSTWAR "PEACE"

*The United States intervention in Lebanon (1958),
Santo Domingo, and South Vietnam . . . as well as the
Russian invasions of Hungary and Czechoslovakia,
indicate the importance attributed to weak states in
the world balance.*[1]

UNEQUALS IN THE POSTWAR WORLD

Hans J. Morgenthau thought the international system left "the
enforcement of the law to the vicissitudes of the distribution of
power between the violator of the law and the victim of the
violation."[2] The neutrality regime adopted at the Hague in 1907
was established for the purpose of giving smaller states the added
strength of an unambiguous law to help withstand stronger
belligerents. Actions that ignore the law detract from its strength
if they go unanswered.

In fact, as discussed in chapter 1, enforcement measures in
international law are automatic and immediate. They are
imposed upon the violator not only by the victim of the violation
but by the entire international community. The effect of this
enforcement, however, is very often so subtle as to remain
imperceptible to the determined violator, and while a definite
price will be paid over the long term, it will not reverse the
offense unless the victim is disposed to seek satisfaction promptly

---

[1]Michael Handel, *Weak States in the International System* (London: Frank
Cass, 1981), 41.

[2]Morgenthau, 282.

and actively. So, the automatic enforcement will, in the case of a weak neutral offended by a belligerent of relative strength, neither restore peace nor deliver justice. This seems to be the true source of Morgenthau's complaint with international law.

As we have seen, even the Charter called upon the coercive use of collective power, including military force, to guarantee the peace and serve justice. During the Cold War, however, the super powers avoided confrontation while there was an increasing tendency for smaller states, acting on their own or as surrogates of their super-power patrons, to take actions that threatened or broke the international peace. The behavior of the United States during this period almost never remained impartial for any significant period of time after hostilities broke out anywhere in the world. National interests dictated policy decisions not impartial in most situations.

In most armed conflicts between smaller states the belligerents found they had to endure the interference of some great power and hope that it would abstain from the introduction of combat forces:

> The fact that the United States is sufficiently powerful to be able to pursue the course which it believes is correct without fear of being held to account by one or the other of the belligerents may make its position easier in practice but it does not dispose of the legal contradictions.[3]

In fact, good policy (which is neutral as far as being noncombatant) partial to one or another belligerent remains inconsistent with the law of neutrality. So these same partial acts, regardless of their salutary effect, give rise to the right of diplomatic protest or even the right to act against the United States with force.

Being just and right is simply not the same as being neutral. While the United States has enjoyed benefits that in practice were identical to neutral rights, these were not rights but privileges arising from fear of more direct employment of U.S. power, not respect for the law of neutrality.

---

[3]Fenwick, 4.

James Cable documents over 40 cases of the United States using of naval forces in implied or direct threats of military force to influence the decisionmaking process of some other state since the end of World War II. He believes that the desired results were forthcoming in over 75 percent of the cases.[4] These cases have rarely resulted in attacks against U.S. forces, fostering an insidious sort of self-deception. It is easy to believe the law stands behind you when your efforts in a just cause are successful, but this is wrong thinking because the Hague neutrality regime does not deal in terms of justice. Its objective was to preserve the peace in third states. The laws of war and neutrality are structured to restrain the use of force in war, not to evaluate or regulate the justice of war.

More than self-deception and wrong thinking, the situations can be more objectively assessed by considering the perspective of those considered to be unjust or aggressors. To start with, they sometimes believe they are righting wrongs perpetrated against them and frequently believe their actions are just, or at least justified. They might view the United States as ignoring its commitment to observe neutral duties under Hague 1907 or violating its commitment in Article 2 (4) of the Charter to refrain from the threat or use of force.

It is illogical to consider the "successes" of the threat or use of force without acknowledging the costs as well as the benefits, especially true if the premise of the automatic enforcement of international law is understood. Because the entire international community participates in the enforcement of the law, the perception of the entire community regarding a state's

---

[4]James Cable, *Gunboat Diplomacy 1919-1979*, 2nd ed., (New York: St. Martin's Press, 1981), 222-258. The numbers of cases considered are undoubtedly based on very conservative estimates of the number of uses of naval forces. Maritime Strategy briefings in Washington generally acknowledge over two hundred cases of U.S. "crisis response" since 1945 and claim naval forces played a role in 80 percent of the cases. Of course, the long range effects of a "successful" show of force may not be as beneficial and can cancel the short-term benefits. Another empirical study of the use of force short of war is found in Barry M. Bleckman and Stephen S. Kaplan, *Force Without War: U.S. Armed Forces as a Political Instrument*, (Washington: Brookings, 1978).

compliance or violation of the law determines the enforcement. This may well result in inconsistent or bifurcated enforcement decisions by the community where its members' perceptions vary, and those decisions may be colored by extra-legal policy considerations that include issues from ideology to economics. While inclusion of such considerations may well diminish the objectivity of the enforcers of the law, they do not diminish the law itself (or the pragmatic rules of behavior which underlie the law).

STILL IN FORCE

The legal status of naval forces employed to influence the actions of another state in the post-World War II "peace" was examined by the International Court of Justice in the *Corfu Channel Case.*

The United Kingdom sent four warships through the channel between Corfu Island and the coast of Albania to assert the right of vessels to use those waters to transit between two areas of the high seas, a right Albania denied existed. The ships, anticipating trouble, were at battle stations as they transited the channel through Albania's territorial waters. Regarding the right of British ships to transit territorial waters at battle stations the Court said, "The intention must have (been), not only to test Albania's attitude but . . . *to demonstrate such force that she would abstain from firing again on passing ships. . . .* (T)he Court is unable to characterize these measures . . . as a violation of Albania's sovereignty." (emphasis added)[5] The message here is that armed suasion is legally acceptable to assert the willingness to defend a right being challenged. The Court went on, however, to make clear such action was only legitimate when it did not violate another's legal rights.

During the transit, two of the destroyers suffered severe damage from a freshly laid minefield. The United Kingdom then set afoot an operation to remove the mines from Albanian waters. The Court was less receptive to this use of naval forces:

> The Court can only regard the alleged right of intervention as

---

[5]ICJ *Report (1949),* 31.

the manifestation of a policy of force, such as has in the past given rise to most serious abuses and as such cannot, whatever be the present defects in international organisation, find a place in international law. Intervention . . . from the nature of things . . . would be reserved for the most powerful states, and might easily lead to perverting the administration of international justice itself.[6]

So, while coercive force was appropriate to assert a right and protect its execution, intervention was held inappropriate (at least as a remedy of first recourse) to correct an injury already suffered.   This would give the majority of U.S. naval demonstrations a clearly legal character under the law of peace.

The situation is not as clear, however, when those same naval forces are used to demonstrate U.S. attitudes regarding an armed conflict, already underway or imminent, between third parties. In these cases the law of peace is rolled aside in favor of (or at least to operate in concert with) the laws of armed conflict that must be understood to include neutral duties. Of course, the United States remains free to behave partially, but from a legal standpoint a state behaving partially regarding belligerents cannot expect to be immune from attack.

The type of confusing situation that can ensue was illustrated during the Korean War, which, in the eyes of many, avoided the legal label "war" but was clearly conducted by both sides with little question that the rules of warfare were in operation.

The People's Republic of China asserted its forces were "volunteers," freed from the direction of the PRC, to attempt to preserve China's formal neutrality. Likewise, The New York Times reported an exchange at Panmunjon when the North Korean delegate defended the neutrality of the Soviet Union asking, "Is your side now at war with the Soviet Union? . . . If not, how can your side deny that the Soviet Union is a neutral nation apart from the two belligerents?" In fact, because there is no recognized intermediate status between peace and war, and the United Nations did not make the necessary policy decisions to respond to Soviet departures from their neutral duties, the Soviets

---

[6]*ICJ Report* (1949), 35.

did not become belligerents and remained technically neutral. The Chinese position, on the other hand, was a legal fiction because their forces were actively engaged in combat under the direction of, carrying out the policy of, and supplied by the government of the PRC.[7]

The U.N. policy decisions that treated the PRC and the Soviet Union as neutrals during the Korean War responded only to the matters in the tactical and strategic spheres. The United Nations effectively limited the theater of combat, although the U.N. belligerents may have worked a legal fiction of their own.[8]

So, the law remains as written, belligerents and neutrals alike incurring legal obligations that, if not fulfilled, give rise to rights of enforcement that include the use of force by the others. Policy decisions not to assert such rights do not change the law or diminish those rights.

THE SUEZ CRISIS

Few ongoing situations are as complex as the Arab-Israeli Wars, which frequently have involved major power centers of the world but never in a more confused environment than the Suez Crisis. Traditional alignments were cast to the winds as national interests dictated British and French policies the United States opposed. And, while the Soviets threatened to enter the fighting against the British and French, the United States pondered how it might avoid taking the same course—and how to stop the Soviets.[9]

---

[7]These forces were much like, but—because of the control and support noted—not identical to, the U.S. "volunteers" who fought for China against Japan before the U.S. entry into World War II, see Spector, 325.

[8]Lauterpacht, 223; *ASIL* 1968, (Judge) R. R. Baxter, 73; Jessup, 98-99. Further, "United Nations forces refrained throughout the conflict from pursuing belligerent aircraft over . . . Soviet territory for fear . . . there was no right of 'hot pursuit' into neutral territory. Similarly, when the United States suggested a naval blockade of the PRC by the United Nations, other United Nations belligerents resisted such action successfully on the same ground." Patrick M. Norton, "Between the Ideology and the Reality: The Shadow of the Law of Neutrality", *Harvard International Law Review* 17 (1976), 266.

[9]For a fairly comprehensive and authoritative treatment see Dwight D. Eisenhower, *The White House Years*, (Garden City, NY: Doubleday and Company, 1965), II:20-57, 69-80, 84-99; Ronald Steel, *Walter Lippmann and*

In this environment ships of the Sixth Fleet found themselves conducting noncombatant evacuations during some of the heaviest fighting of the conflict from 31 October through 2 November 1956. The small fast transport *BURDO*, and the destroyers *HARLAN R. DICKSON*, and *HUGH PURVIS* went into Haifa as the Israelis engaged the Egyptian destroyer *IBRAHIM EL AWAL* just outside the port. The attack transport *CAMBRIA* also found herself off the Gaza strip evacuating United Nations truce observers whose position was under fire. And, in the worst situation of all, the attack transport *CHILTON*, the attack cargo ship *THUBAN*, and the destroyers *CHARLES S. SPERRY* and *ALLEN M. SUMNER* accompanying the amphibious force ship *FORT SNELLING* made an uninvited approach on Alexandria to conduct the evacuation there. Once inside the harbor nearly 40 air raids, opposed by heavy anti-aircraft fire, occurred in the immediate vicinity of these ships, with shells passing directly over *CHILTON*. Then, upon sortie on 2 November, during yet another air raid on the port, force commander Commodore Laing was confronted with taking over 4500 non-combatants through an inadequately swept minefield.[10] Regarding his guidance the Commodore reported:

> I'd had no instructions about shooting back and thereby upsetting the international applecart but good. I told Admiral Brown (Commander Sixth Fleet) I'd play that by ear. I am not

---

the American Century (Boston and Toronto: Little, Brown, and Company, 1980), 505-508; see also Donald Neff, *Warriors at Suez* (New York: Simon & Schuster, 1981) especially chapters XVIII and XIX; for a British perspective see James L. Stokesbury, *Navy and Empire* (New York: William Morrow and Co., 1983), 399-401; regarding the United Nations Emergency Force, David W. Wainhouse, et al., *International Peace Observation* (Baltimore and London: The Johns Hopkins Press, 1966), 277-279; also Indar Jit Rikhye, et al, *The Thin Blue Line: International Peacekeeping and Its Future* (New Haven and London: Yale University Press, 1974), 48-53.

[10]Thomas A. Bryson, *Tars, Turks, and Tankers: The Role of the United States Navy in the Middle East, 1800-1979(Metuchin, NJ: The Scarecrow Press, Inc., 1980), 109-117. None of this data ever showed up in The New York Times* although there was extensive daily reporting of the other (foreign force) activities throughout the period. Perhaps security or other classification concerns kept this data out of the press at the time.

sure that he had any instructions in the matter. It was one of damnedest international situations I'd ever heard about and I don't really think it has ever existed before. . . . If anybody got tough and gave me any more trouble than I was already having—like lead bullets—I was going to toss a few back and then go to sit around a long green table (at inquiry or court martial).[11]

Fortunately, the ships were not directly engaged. If they had been, the Commodore apparently had the right idea about how to respond. It seems that Chief of Naval Operations Admiral Arleigh Burke had told Admiral Brown concisely, "If United States citizens are in danger protect them. Take no guff from anyone."[12] It is worrisome that the guidance apparently was not shared with the on scene commander!

JUSTICE AT THE EXPENSE OF PEACE?

At his inauguration, President Kennedy asked that the United States might, "join in a new endeavor . . . a new world of law, where the strong are just and the weak secure."[13] Exactly what the new president meant is probably lost to history, but his actions in office indicate he intended to offer U.S. strength to serve the (unneutral, not impartial) purpose of justice and thus secure a just world for the weak, even at the expense of peace. Three months later, on 20 April 1961, his brother Robert, the Attorney General, told the press:

> The neutrality laws are among the oldest laws in our statute books. Most of the provisions date from the first years of our independence and, with only minor revisions, have continued in force since the 18th Century. Clearly they were not designed for the kind of situation which exists in the world today.[14]

---

[11]Ibid., 115.

[12]Ibid., 108.

[13]John F. Kennedy, *Public Papers of the Presidents of the United States* (Washington: GPO, 1962), 2.

[14]The Attorney General (Kennedy), statement to the press, Apr. 20, 1961, MS. Dept. of State, file 711.34/4-2161 quoted at Whiteman, 11, 231.

Reading between the lines here one sees Robert Kennedy making exactly the same kind of statement Mahan reportedly made at the 1899 Hague Conference. The United States, with global interests and perspectives, was no longer best served by a policy of strict neutrality.

A few days before the Attorney General's statement, the United States had witnessed from close range the decimation of an abortive invasion force on the beaches of Cuba at the Bay of Pigs. Planned during the previous administration, the invasion force had been trained and supplied by the United States. The CIA even promised the invaders that the U.S. Navy would protect seaborne forces.[15]

A large U.S. task force was in place off the coast of Cuba when the invasion occurred, but President Kennedy refused to allow it to join the hostilities even long enough to rescue the forces it had escorted to the beach. When failure was clear, U.S. destroyers attempted to assist in an evacuation. In doing so they found themselves well within the range of Castro's guns, which were butchering the landing force. Only the destroyer *EATON* was fired upon. A Cuban tank took her under fire, shooting twice, missing both times—but not by much, the rounds bracketing the ship.[16] Destroyermen understood that situation, and it was not good. Without significant maneuvering, only a mistake by the enemy gun crew could avoid a hit by the next round. Apparently, although President Kennedy would have been happy to have Castro removed from power by force by Cuban rebels, even with U.S. support, he was unprepared to go to war with Cuba openly. After hours of discouraging reports on the deteriorating situation, Kennedy denied another request from Chief of Naval Operations Arleigh Burke to use naval forces at the scene to help the invasion force saying, "Burke, I don't want the United States involved in this."[17] Admiral Burke was greatly distressed and attempted to drive home the facts of the situation

---

[15]Cable, *Gunboat*, 238; Peter Wyden, *Bay of Pigs: The Untold Story* (New York: Simon & Schuster, 1979), 78. Wyden's book is apparently written from declassified reports and first hand accounts.

[16]Wyden, 264, 282.

[17]Ibid., 270.

to his Commander in Chief by raising his voice and saying, "Hell, Mr. President . . . we are involved!"[18]

Less than a year after Kennedy's death, U.S. forces were trying to prevent a Communist victory in South Vietnam through blatantly overt support:

Units of the Seventh Fleet were operating off the coast of Vietnam. Among other things, they were conducting an intelligence collection mission in support of the South Vietnamese. U.S. forces had never engaged the North Vietnamese. Then, on 1 August 1964, three North Vietnamese motor torpedo boats pursued South Vietnamese vessels into international waters. The North Vietnamese encountered U.S.S. *MADDOX* on a surveillance mission, made the false assumption she was directly supporting the South Vietnamese vessels, and proceeded to attack her. During the engagement *MADDOX* sank one of the patrol boats.[19]

Three days later, a similar but much more confused nighttime incident occurred. *MADDOX* was again involved, but another destroyer, *TURNER JOY,* was the primary target of the somewhat questionable attack.[20] Together these episodes became known as the Gulf of Tonkin incident. In response, the United States attacked targets in North Vietnam and plunged headlong into the tragic conflict that consumed the nation's energies, options, treasure, and young for the next decade.[21]

Any similarity between the assumed attack on *MAINE* and

---

[18]Ibid. Perhaps President Kennedy chose to limit that involvement to the unneutral service rendered to Cuban Anti-Castro forces, and to intervene in Cuban internal affairs from afar. That was certainly the effect of his decision. The other possibility was that in his concern not to spread the disaster, which was ongoing at that point, to include the regular forces of the United States and to retain some semblance of "plausible deniability" he had not thought through the depth of U.S. involvement and the price being paid by those on the beach.

[19]"U.S. Defense Department Reports 3 North Vietnamese PT Boats Fired at U.S. Destroyer *MADDOX*, On routine Patrol, in International Waters 30 Miles Off North Vietnam in Gulf of Tonkin", *The New York Times,* 3 August 1964, 1:8.

[20]"U.S. Defense Department Reports North Vietnamese PT Boats Attacked 2 Destroyers, Tonkin Gulf", *The New York Times,* 5 August 1964, 1:4.

[21] Whiteman, 12, 128-133; Manchester, 2:1245.

the declaration of war against Spain in 1898, the arrest of crew members from *DOLPHIN* and the Senate resolution on the "Tampico Incident" justifying occupation of Veracruz in 1914; the attack on *GREER* by the submarine that believed it was firing in self-defense and the "shoot on sight" order in 1941; and the unclear attacks on *MADDOX* and *TURNER JOY* and the "Gulf of Tonkin Resolution" might be attributed to the fact the chief executive had abandoned impartiality in each of the cases. Some would say, these events, whatever their true nature, were handy tools for a President who knew beforehand what he wanted to do.

Before the United States could extricate herself from Vietnam she found mere suspicion of unneutral conduct by the United States was sufficient to move some nations to assert belligerent rights against her forces.

In June 1967, during an eruption of the Arab-Israeli War, the Israelis bombed, strafed, and torpedoed the electronic intelligence ship *U.S.S. LIBERTY* in international waters in the Eastern Mediterranean.[22] "*U.S.S. LIBERTY (AGTR-5)* was an ear to the world in general and the United States in particular that had to be deafened if the Israeli plan (to defeat Egypt) were to succeed."[23]

The mission of electronic intelligence was becoming an increasingly unacceptable reminder of U.S. partiality when conducted by ships close to belligerent shores, as the *PUEBLO* Incident would prove. The war in Korea has not ended. An

---

[22]"Communications Ship *U.S.S. LIBERTY* Attacked by Mistake by Israeli Planes and Torpedo Boats in International Waters About 15 Miles North of Sinai," *The New York Times*, 9 June 1967, 1:6.

[23]RADM Kemp Tolley, U.S. Navy (Ret.) Letter published in "Comment and Discussion", *United States Naval Institute Proceedings (USNIP)*, September 1979, 24-27. Admiral Tolley asserted the attack was purposeful and attributed his information to a diplomat serving in the area at the time. Chaim Herzog, on the other hand, acknowledges claims like Admiral Tolley's have been made but dismisses them explaining *LIBERTY* looked like an Egyptian ship to pilots attacking her at high speed. This might be credible, despite the superb reputation of Israeli pilots, but Herzog fails to explain the machine gun and torpedo attacks made at close range by Israeli PT boats. Chaim Herzog, *The Arab-Israeli Wars* (New York: Random House, 1982), 178. See also Cable, *Gunboat*, 244. Although Israel paid reparation the claim of mis-identification was never withdrawn leaving the motivations and facts of this example in dispute.

armistice was signed to suspend hostilities. Legally the status is still undeclared war subject to the restrictions agreed to at Panmunjom. The partiality of the United States has never been in question there. U.S. forces stationed in South Korea are still committed to its defense.

In January 1968, North Korea attacked and seized the *U.S.S. PUEBLO. PUEBLO* was in international waters on an intelligence mission.[24] The North Korean attack set in motion one of the most humiliating episodes of U.S. history and serves as fair warning of what could happen elsewhere because, as Professor Daniel P. O'Connell explained the situation, "North Korea exploited a local and momentary advantage against a victim otherwise incomparably more powerful."[25]

The United States may have held the preponderance of power, but North Korea did not stand alone. In 1961 Pyongyang signed a mutual defense treaty with the Soviet Union, and in the opinion of Abram Shulsky, regardless of the Soviet assessment of the seizure of the *PUEBLO*, that country would have been hard pressed to permit the use of U.S. force against an ally so embarrassingly close to their own territory.[26]

In response to the seizure of *PUEBLO* the United States sent *ENTERPRISE, YORKTOWN, RANGER*, and their supporting task groups to the North Korean coast:

Together they constituted the largest naval force assembled in

---

[24]"North Korean Patrol Boats Seize U.S. Navy Intelligence Ship *PUEBLO* Off Wonson, Take Vessel and Crew of 83 into North Korean Port", *The New York Times*, 24 January 1968, 1:8.

[25]O'Connell, 6; Cable, *Gunboat*, 50, 245; see also Alfred P. Rubin, "Some Legal Implications of the *PUEBLO* Incident", *International and Comparative Law Quarterly* 18 (1969), 961-970, for an analysis of the unnecessary surrender of the previous U.S. position on both the breadth of the territorial sea and the concept of what is acceptable as "innocent passage".

[26]Abram M. Shulsky, "Coercive Diplomacy," in Bradford Dismukes and James M. McConnell, eds., *Soviet Naval Diplomacy* (New York: Pergamon, 1979), 119. The Soviets had spent 6 years after the Cuban Missile Crisis trying to prevent another humiliation while supporting an ally. They still had problems projecting power far from their shores but they had no excuse for not being able operate within one day's steaming time from their own bases (and less than an hour by air).

response to a crisis since the Cuban missile crisis of 1962. . . .
When the crisis began a (Soviet) scientific research/intelligence
ship and a *RIGA* destroyer escort were on patrol in the
Tsushima Strait, and these two units met the incoming
ENTERPRISE task group as it entered the Sea of Japan on
January 24. They were joined at the end of January by a
SAM-KOTLIN (class) destroyer, an SSM-equipped *KILDEN*
(class) destroyer, and an intelligence collector.[27]

Despite the buildup, U.S. and Soviet units soon withdrew
when it became apparent that North Korean concessions
regarding *PUEBLO* or her crew would not be forthcoming. The
only incident during the demonstration, after *PUEBLO*'s seizure,
was the ramming of a U.S. destroyer by a Soviet merchant
vessel. Whether this was intentional is not known; the vessel,
however, did not have the right of way and the incident followed
a series of at least 11 violations of the rules of the road by Soviet
vessels at the scene.[28]

Campaigning in 1968, Richard Nixon said, "Unless the United
States reacts . . . you are going to have more *PUEBLO*s" . . .
less than three months after he entered the White House . . .
the North Koreans shot down (a Navy EC-121 communications
intelligence plane with 31 men aboard) killing all hands.[29]

NEW JERSEY and a task force which from time to time involved
a number of carriers entered the Sea of Japan a week later.
North Korea ignored them and they eventually were withdrawn.
Their influence on later North Korean decisions can neither be
known nor discounted.[30]

---

[27]Ibid., 121. "SAM" indicates surface to air missile capability. "SSM"
indicates surface to surface missile capability.

[28]Ibid.

[29]Manchester, 2:1444-1445. See also "North Korea Claims to Have
Downed a U.S. Navy Reconnaissance Plane Which It Says Intruded Into Its
Airspace", *The New York Times*, 16 April 1969, 1:8-14:5.

[30]Cable, *Gunboat*, 247.

THE NIXON DOCTRINE

> Foreign governments are free to accept pronouncements of the executive authority with which they deal as expressive of the will of the state.[31]

Since the end of World War II, the United States often has placed naval forces near the scene of armed conflicts where our bias and intent to influence the belligerents were clear. Not all belligerents have refrained from extending the hostilities to U.S. forces. Yet the Nixon Doctrine, while purporting to shift the responsibility for protecting friendly countries from the forces of United States to those of the endangered countries, continued to assert that the United States would be involved in the defense of allies and friends. At the time of its pronouncement, President Nixon summarized the doctrine:

> Unless a major power intervened in a Third World conflict, the United States should not commit its combat forces. We should provide military and economic aid to friendly states in whatever amounts necessary to defeat Soviet-supported insurgents, but the country under attack must undertake the responsibility for providing the troops to mount its own defenses. If a country cannot mobilize the capability and the will to fight after receiving our aid and training, sending our own troops to do the fighting would at best provide only temporary success. Once we withdrew the enemy would take over.[32]

Close examination of this statement could lead to the conclusion that the United States was embarking on a course of unneutral conduct in situations where states had already resorted to combat but that were deemed inappropriate to risk the involvement of U.S. forces as a matter of policy. If that unneutral conduct increases the risk of being drawn into the conflict, this policy would prove self-defeating. Therefore, the

---

[31]*ASIL* (1967), Quincy Wright, 52.

[32]Richard Nixon, *1999: Victory Without War* (New York: Simon & Schuster, 1988), 122-123.

Nixon Doctrine, viewed in light of global interests and interdependence, really didn't change anything for naval forces.

In essence, the doctrine is not far from what George Washington said about where the United States should get involved—if you make the assumption that treaties reflect interests.[33] Further, once a treaty is concluded, keeping good faith with it is in the national interest, so even if U.S. ground forces were employed more conservatively, the doctrine could not be expected to foster a change in traditional naval force employment patterns, or the naval policy they reflect. Naval forces are frequently used in presence—or suasion—missions off the coasts of warring nations where our ground forces are not involved.

THE 1971 INDO-PAKISTANI WAR

The full impact of the dangers of the Nixon Doctrine may be seen in light of U.S. actions to influence the Indo-Pakistani War beginning in December 1971. In that situation the legal distinctions between the applicability of the law of war and the law of peace were clear, yet the policy of the United States continued to either ignore or accept the threat of being drawn into war.

As Elihu Lauterpacht pointed out, the Middle East and India-Pakistan conflicts were clearly understood to be "war" and as such, the states involved have dealt with the law of war in technical terms including the operation of prize courts.[34]

The animosity between India and Pakistan dated back to their inception when British colonial rule ended in 1947. On 9 August 1971, the Soviets entered into a 20-year friendship pact,

---

[33]"It is folly in one nation to look for disinterested favors from another." From Washington's Farewell Address, Richardson, I, 205-216.

[34]*ASIL* (1968), Elihu Lauterpacht, 60-61. In this work, "Middle East conflicts" means the Arab-Israeli wars, the internal situation in Lebanon, and the problems which arose within the Persian Gulf region, but does not include the acts of terrorism throughout the region.

a kind of alliance, with India.[35] Pakistan was allied with the United States by virtue of membership in the South East Asia Treaty Organization (SEATO).[36]

These alliances became a connection that threatened world peace when India declared war on Pakistan in December of 1971.[37] The U.S. response to this situation, according to then National Security Advisor and later Secretary of State Henry Kissinger, was not only related to SEATO and the Nixon Doctrine, but also to Kissinger's efforts at the time to open a more productive relationship with China. So from the U.S. viewpoint, motivation to influence the outcome was driven not only by our alliance commitment but perhaps even more by policy concerns in support of broader U.S. interests.[38]

From the Indian viewpoint, however, the traditional support of the United States evidenced by the existence of the SEATO link with Pakistan, and the concurrent redeployment of U.S.

---

[35]"India and U.S.S.R. Sign 20-Yr. Friendship Treaty Intended to Deter Pakistan from Attacking India," *The New York Times*, 10 August 1971, 1:2. "U.S.S.R. Ratifies 20-Yr. Friendship Treaty With India and Warns It Will Take 'Urgently Effective Measures' to Protect India from Attack," *The New York Times*, 14 August 1971, 6:1. Henry Kissinger wrote: "What had caused the war, in Nixon's view and mine . . . was India's determination to use the crisis to establish its preeminence on the subcontinent. . . . The Soviet Union could have restrained India; it chose not to. It had, in fact, actively encouraged war by signing the Friendship Treaty." Henry Kissinger, *The White House Years*, (Boston: Little, Brown & Co., 1979), 885.

[36]TIAS 3170. The pact was supposed to protect Pakistan against communist aggression (according to a unilateral declaration by the United States -- Article 4 of the treaty is unequivocal regarding "armed attack" in the treaty area) but Kissinger's interpretation transcended the words of the treaty. He explained: "The victim of the attack was an ally -- however reluctant many were to admit it -- to which we had made several explicit promises concerning precisely this contingency. Clear treaty commitments reinforced by other undertakings dated back to 1959." Kissinger, 886. (A bilateral defense agreement was concluded in 1959). Interestingly, Pakistan withdrew from SEATO in 1972.

[37]"Text of Ghandi Statement", *The New York Times*, 4 December 1971, 10:6.

[38]Kissinger, chapter XXI, passim; Kenneth R. McGruther, "The Role of Perception in Naval Diplomacy", *NWCR*, September-October 1974, 7; Marvin Kalb and Bernard Kalb, *Kissinger* (Boston: Little, Brown & Co., 1974), 259; Bailey, 934.

warships from their stations off Vietnam to the Indian Ocean in response to the war was a matter of grave concern. This was especially true once the United States declared, by leaking high-level meeting minutes to the media, an intention to "tilt"[39] in favor of Pakistan.

India, an ally of the Soviet Union, had formally declared war on an ally of the United States, Pakistan. As Grotius explained alliance relationships, this might have been interpreted by India to have already brought the United States into war. Consider his example: "Upon war being declared upon Antiochus, there was no occasion for a separate declaration against the Aetolians, who had openly joined Antiochus. For . . . the Aetolians had, by that act voluntarily brought war upon themselves."[40] Henry Kissinger acknowledged that this aspect of the situation was consciously considered and even called it to the attention of India in an attempt to dissuade them from further action.[41] The administration apparently decided to cast caution to the winds: "The war led to record deployment levels (in the Indian Ocean) . . . 14 combatants and auxiliaries for the (United States), 26 for the Soviets."[42]

The official "tilt" of the United States assumed the restraint of India, a tremendous act of faith. Again the United States openly acted with partiality against a state formally at war for the purpose of achieving its policy objectives. Such U.S. interference would certainly violate her impartiality even in the absence of direct military assistance to Pakistan. The United States forces, therefore, must have been considered a potential threat by Indian forces. India might have even considered the need to take

---

[39]Kissinger, 897.

[40]Grotius, Book III, chapter III, Section IX, 320-321. Though the war was not communist aggression, India could have interpreted the Kissinger interpretation of SEATO link (if known to them), the Nixon Doctrine, and the "tilt" statement to mean the United States was behaving as an ally of Pakistan.

[41]According to Kissinger, Nixon told a Soviet Minister visiting the United States at the time, "The Soviet Union has a treaty with India; we have one with Pakistan. You must recognize the urgency of a cease-fire and political settlement of the crisis." Kissinger,. 904.

[42]James M. McConnell and Anne Kelly Calhoun, "The December 1971 Indo-Pakistani Crisis" in Dismukes and McConnell, 178.

defensive action against such a threat without waiting to absorb the first hit. Ignoring the broader policy considerations that presumably restrained India, the best tactical option available to India might have been to conduct a pre-emptive strike against the *ENTERPRISE* task force. Such action was mentioned but it is impossible to determine the degree of plausibility attached to such a drastic alternative by India.[43]

Was this a real option for India? The United States must not have thought so, but an examination of the facts calls that assessment into question, at least from the tactical standpoint. Sea denial forces available to India could have threatened or in a worst case scenario partially removed, at least temporarily, the combat capability of the U.S. naval forces on station and, in the Indian view, charged with executing the "tilt". Consider the following situation which did result from Indian action:

> On the night of 3-4 December there was an engagement about twenty miles from Karachi in which the Pakistani destroyer *KHAIBAR* was sunk by Styx missiles fired from an *OSA*-class boat. On that night the Liberian-registered *S.S. VENUS CHALLENGER*, whose estimated date of arrival at Karachi was 5 December, disappeared. On 5 January her wreck was discovered by the Pakistani navy 26.5 miles from Karachi. She lay in shallow water on an even keel with derricks visible about six feet above mean high tide, and bore evidence of having been struck forward of the bridge by a missile, with consequent heavy damage. Subsequent investigation showed that she was lost on the night of the sinking of the *KHAIBAR*.[44]

In times past, the loss of the *S.S. VENUS CHALLENGER*, which went with no survivors, would have been sufficient to

---

[43]"If the American aircraft carrier *ENTERPRISE* dares to intervene . . . a member of the Indian Parliament said . . . 'the Government should not hesitate to blast it out of the water.'" Quoted in Fox Butterworth, "U.S. Ships With Dual Role Moving Up Bay of Bengal: Indian Animosity Grows", *The New York Times*, 16 December 1971, 1:7; "The remedies available to an aggrieved belligerent as a consequence of the neutral's failure to fulfill its obligations range from the demand for moral or material reparation to the taking of retaliatory measures." Tucker, 261.

[44]O'Connell, 86-87.

threaten world peace—remember the U.S. responses to losses of neutral merchant ships before the two world wars. But she was sailing under a Liberian flag of convenience. The threat to the freedom of the seas and the property loss were insignificant to Liberia who could have done little militarily were she moved to indignation. This phenomenon contributed to the speed with which Indian naval forces proved successful. "By December 6 or 7 . . . . Both East and West Pakistan had been effectively blockaded."[45]

The danger of unintended escalation was real: "An Indian show of force would have exacerbated an already tense situation, since Indian *FOXTROT*-class submarines were, as far as U.S. observers knew, indistinguishable from those that the USSR had already deployed to the scene."[46]

The conflict witnessed Soviet-built missile boats, operated by

---

[45]McConnell and Calhoun, 184. The term "blockade" seems not to be applied here as a legal term of art. The authors likely mean that the Indians had achieved command of the seas in the vicinity of the Pakistani coast. The United States did engage the issue of Indian behavior regarding U.S. flag merchant ships. *BUCKEYE STATE* had been the victim of an Indian air attack and another ship was intercepted by an Indian naval vessel. Secretary of State William P. Rogers complained to the Indian Ambassador about the incidents which also occurred on 5 December.

U.S. owned—but not U.S. flag ships—also warranted U.S. diplomatic action and the threat of "whatever measures were necessary" that month. Cuban gunboats seized the Panamanian flag, Miami based merchant ship *LALIA EXPRESS* near the Bahamas over 100 miles from the Cuban coast on that same 5 December. Her sister ship, *JOHNNY EXPRESS*, was attacked and then seized by gunboats on 15 December about 120 miles from Cuba. The Captain, Jose Villa—a naturalized U.S. citizen was wounded in the attack. The two ships crews totaled 27 men. The State Department protested the seizures and threatened the action mentioned above on 17 December. Cuba claimed the ships were carrying arms to anti-Cuban forces. In April of 1972 U.S. warships in the Caribbean were instructed to assist *any* friendly state's merchant ships which were interfered with by Cuba as a result of the incidents. See Commander J. B. Finklestein, U.S. Navy, "Naval and Maritime Events July 1971—December 1971", *USNIP*, May 1972, 352, and Commander J. B Finklestein, U.S. Navy, "Naval and Maritime Events January 1972—June 1972", *USNIP*, May 1973, 56. Commander Finklestein does not report the resolution of the incidents.

[46]McGruther, 7.

Indians, attacking a Pakistani destroyer at night in an assault so indiscriminate that a civilian merchant ship was accidentally destroyed as well. The danger to U.S. ships was not imaginary. Direct combat between the super powers was a real danger that could have resulted from an accident of war. The alliance and neutrality issues addressed worsened the danger for an accidental or misinterpreted engagement being considered purposeful by providing a logical rationale.

The experiences of *PANAY*, *LIBERTY*, and *PUEBLO* were the result of essentially unarmed warships, operating close to a "war," being exploited to the advantage of smaller states that believed the United States would not attack them in reprisal. (Perhaps we will always wonder if *STARK* should be added to this list).[47] Kissinger wrote,

> However unlikely an American military move against India, the other side could not be sure; it might not be willing to accept even the minor risk that we might act irrationally. It was the best means to split the Soviet Union and India. Moscow was prepared to harass us; it was in our judgment not prepared to run military risks. Moving the carrier task force into the Bay of Bengal committed us to no final act, but it created precisely the margin of uncertainty needed to force a decision (not to dismember West Pakistan) by New Delhi and Moscow.[48]

---

[47]"Iraqi Sources Confirm *STARK* Attacked Deliberately", *Defense & Foreign Affairs Weekly*, May 22-28, 1989, 8. Although this report was unsubstantiated (and is not given much credibility among naval officers) it does raise the possibility the attack was not an accident -- or if it was it was seen as beneficial by some in Iraq. The report alleged the pilot of the attacking craft was given high honors and bonuses for the successful execution of the "planned operation." The Iraqi motive allegedly was to punish the United States for closer ties with Iran. In a conversation with Ambassador David Newton, who was posted in Baghdad at the time of the attack, made clear that his contact with the Iraqis left him with the impression that the representatives he spoke with believed it was an accident. Of course, such a decision would have been made by Saddam Hussein who is famous for neither his trustworthiness nor his candor with other Iraqis.

[48]Kissinger, 912. See also Gaddis, 300. Obviously, this effort failed to protect the territorial integrity of Pakistan.

"Irrational" is right. That very uncertainty is a double-edged sword. While the United States might righteously and correctly regard its naval forces in these situations as the cutting edge of the sword of freedom, the other side has a sword that is getting sharper all the time. Today technology has allowed smaller states to obtain potent "sea denial" forces that could raise the stakes of the naval demonstration game to unacceptable levels. We must now frequently endanger our forces to gain their deterrent effect.[49] The "decision" we forced instead could have proven "the risk of irrational action" had India confronted the U.S. forces instead of (presumably) being influenced by them. Remember the local power equation could easily have been evaluated by India to favor India, especially at sea. And the "margin of uncertainty" must have burdened the minds of the naval unit commanders on the U.S. ships as well.

THE BLOODY LEBANESE "PEACE"

In mid-1983, U.S. forces that had been sent into Lebanon earlier as part of an international peacekeeping force were being attacked more and more. The intention of their deployment was to stabilize the situation, deterring future fighting by bringing the power and influence of the U.S., British, French, and Italian governments to bear. Actually, it was U.S. forces again asserting neutrality attempted to influence the outcome of a civil war and hundreds of servicemen died or were wounded in a failed effort.

Forces in opposition to the Gemayal government in Lebanon already considered their issues important enough to kill and die for. Outside efforts to stabilize the situation frustrated those ends. The situation was very confused and involved irregular and factional forces opposing the largely Christian government. By the end of August, Druse, Shi'a, and Syrian statements reflect

---

[49]Consider this contribution to the literature by Commodore K. R. Menon, Indian Navy: "The supremacy of the supercarrier battle group may not be in question in a shooting war, but the use of large forces in low-intensity conflicts could change if the threshold of losses sustained by a superpower navy were to increase to unacceptable levels because of the introduction of missile armed air-independent submarines." K. R. Menon, Commodore, Indian Navy, "Third World Navies React", *USNIP*, March 1989, 94.

that they considered the U.S. Marines part of the "enemy." They thought the United States had taken sides with the government forces. Then, in September, in response to stepped up sniping against the peacekeepers and artillery attacks against the Lebanese Army, President Reagan authorized the use of naval gunfire support and naval air power to protect the Marines at the Beirut airport. By 13 September, U.S. neutrality was entirely forsaken when the State Department announced the President had authorized Sixth Fleet assets to support the Lebanese Army.[50]

> A few isolated voices questioned . . . whether the nation might be imperceptibly passing an important watershed in Lebanon.
> "They are now apparently there for another purpose," Senator Cranston warned. "The marines' peacekeeping mission has expanded to involve their tacit support for one of the factions . . . in a civil war of decades duration.". . . overthrow of the Lebanese Government would be a severe jolt to American diplomacy. . . . Loss of the Government in Lebanon would cause moderate Arabs . . . to see little benefit to siding with the (United States).[51]

U.S. forces were now a belligerent element. Presidential decisions regarding tactical responses to political concerns altered the legal situation. The stated role of U.S. forces changed from neutral peacekeeping (in Lebanon) to support of partisan objectives deemed to serve broader U.S. national interests.

This significant change was not fully understood. Two weeks later Speaker of the House O'Neill said, "As long as I'm

---

[50]"Key Sections of the Pentagon's Report on Attack on the Marines", *The New York Times*, 29 December 1983, A13:1; Hedrick Smith, "Reagan Upgrading Lebanon Presence", *The New York Times*, 13 September 1983, A1:5; and Hedrick Smith, "Deepened Involvement", *The New York Times*, 14 September 1983, A1:3-4.

[51]Hedrick Smith, "Deepened Involvement", *The New York Times*, 14 September 1983, A1:3-4, A15:1.

here, (an undeclared war) will never happen again".[52] Congress had just voted to permit the Marines to remain in Lebanon for another 18 months, until after the 1984 elections. Despite the analysis and debate that attended this important decision, the Speaker apparently still believed the United States was neutral.

The implication may be that the U.S. Government was playing domestic political games. Actually, an 18-month commitment might have served the U.S. foreign policy well by preventing a divisive debate from taking on a partisan character in the upcoming U.S. presidential and congressional campaigns. The extended authority was a sincere effort to ensure the safety of our peacekeeping forces at Beirut airport. The policy decisions were seen in positive terms by U.S. decisionmakers, but the legal implications of the policy decisions apparently escaped their full consideration.

This is not surprising. After all, the multinational peacekeeping force was originally put into Lebanon in the belief it could deter fighting among Lebanese factions. It was not unreasonable for the same decisionmakers to assume the force was capable of deterring attacks on itself. While not unreasonable, the assumption was as wrong as was the belief it could deter the factions in the civil war. The U.S. forces were now not only complicating efforts to achieve objectives by opposition factions operating against the Lebanese Government, they were also actively working against those objectives. They had taken sides in the conflict and they were going to help deny the goals of those opposing the government. The implications of this would be fully recognized by the United States only in retrospect.

General Paul X. Kelley, then Commandant of the Marine Corps, still believed, as did so many others, that the Marines were not facing "imminent hostilities,"[53] but some did question the wisdom of the evolving U.S. policy in Lebanon. One

---

[52]Steven V. Roberts, "Congress Adopts Measures Allowing Marines in Beirut", *The New York Times*, 30 September 1983, A1:6.

[53]Bernard Gwertzman, "Reagan to Let Marines Give Some Aid to Lebanese Army and European Peace Forces", *The New York Times*, 14 September 1983, A1:6, A14:1.

particularly astute commentary came from columnist James Reston on 18 September, over a month before the infamous attack:

> In the confusion between the President and the Congress over war powers, it has been scarcely noted that in the chaotic military situation in Lebanon, the President has in a way delegated or at least risked his authority, not to the Congress, but to the local marine commanders around Beirut.
>
> Having ordered the marines into the Beirut battle zone, where they are taking casualties, he has instructed them to call for guns and bombers on the U.S. warships off shore to knock out their attackers when, in their judgment, this is necessary—without checking with their military and political superiors in Washington.
>
> But as the attackers are within range of U.S. warships close to the Beirut shore, so are the U.S. warships in range of the Syrian missiles, supplied by the Soviet Union, and the French missiles, now in Syrian possession, that blew British ships out of the water in the battle of the Falklands.[54]

On 8 September, U.S. naval gunfire support was used for the first time in the Lebanon conflict. Fire was called in to defend the Marines against shelling from Druse batteries just south of Beirut. On 17 September, ships fired on targets in the Syrian controlled area of Lebanon for the first time. Syria immediately responded with a warning that Syrian losses would be answered, and orders were issued to Syrian forces to return any fire directed at them. Even more significant was the fact that the 17 September bombardment of antigovernment militia batteries in the Syrian area was the first time U.S. forces were not firing in self-defense; the batteries attacked were not shelling U.S. positions but the Lebanese Defense Ministry. On 19 September another major change occurred. The Lebanese Army undertook an attack against Druse militia and Palestinian forces near the town of Suk al Gharb. When the tide of battle turned against the Lebanese Army, *VIRGINIA* and *JOHN RODGERS* closed the

---

[54]James Reston, "Leave it to the Marines?" *The New York Times*, 18 September 1983, E19:1-4.

beach to a range of a little more than a mile and delivered intense covering fire to minimize Lebanese Army losses and prevent a demoralizing defeat.[55] These actions in the latter half of September put the United States squarely into the war in Lebanon, if for no other reason because, "In naval warfare, the public vessels of a neutral state must refrain from rendering services of any kind to belligerent . . . units."[56]

The regular forces of Syria and the organized forces of the various militias were unquestionably exercising belligerent rights against the *de jure* government of Lebanon. Further, the Gemayal Government was not, treating those forces as domestic criminals but as belligerents. Whether a "war" was believed to exist or not the incidents of armed force were certainly being handled under the "law of war." Consequently, observance of belligerent and neutral rights and duties was appropriate. And, regarding U.S. forces, the legal guidance provided to, but perhaps not consulted by, fleet units at the time indicated that: "If a neutral state does not observe the principle of impartiality, the belligerent influenced by such nonobservance may consider itself to be no longer bound by its obligations toward the neutral."[57]

All the facts entitled the offended belligerents to believe the United States had abandoned neutrality, or at least its protections. After the 23 October truck bomb attack on the Marine Barracks in Beirut killed over 200 marines and sailors, investigators concluded:

> The mission . . . was implicitly characterized as a peacekeeping operation, although "peacekeeping" was not

---

[55]Thomas L. Friedman, "U.S. Warships Fire on Lebanese Area Held by Syrians", *The New York Times*, 18 September 1983, 1:4; Bernard Gwertzman, "No Truce Yet for Reagan in Congress or in Lebanon", *The New York Times*, 18 September 1983, E1:1-2; Bernard Gwertzman, "U.S. Warships Fire in Direct Support of Lebanese Army: Washington View", *The New York Times*, 20 September 1983, A1:5; and E.J. Dionne, Jr., "U.S. Warships Fire in Direct Support of Lebanese Army: Shelling is Heavy", *The New York Times*, 20 September 1983, A1:6.

[56]Tucker, 208.

[57]U.S. Navy Department, *Law of Naval Warfare NWIP 10-2* (Washington, DC: U.S. Navy Department, Office of the C.N.O., 1955), para. 230.

explicit in the mission statement.

Alert and Execute Orders were carefully worded to emphasize . . . a noncombatant role.

By the end of September 1983, the situation in Lebanon had changed to the extent that not one of the initial conditions upon which the mission statement was premised was still valid. The environment clearly was hostile. . . . The image of (U.S. forces), in the eyes of the factional militias, had become pro-Israel, pro-Phalange, and anti-Moslem.

After (U.S. forces) engaged in direct fire support of the (Lebanese Army), a significant portion of the Lebanese population no longer considered the (United States) as a neutral.

Following the U.S. action at Suk al Gharb, hostile acts against (U.S. forces) increased, and the Marines began taking significantly more casualties.[58]

The facts of the situation soon led the Syrians to assert (through actions) their inherent right of self-defense. They must have considered U.S. reconnaissance of the area of Lebanon under Syrian control as an effort to develop intelligence, including targeting data, regarding their positions. This is especially understandable in light of U.S. naval forces supporting the Lebanese Army against groups Syria must have considered as "allies" and delivery of naval bombardment inside the Syrian controlled area. Consequently, the Syrians made good their threat to retaliate and fired upon U.S. carrier-based aircraft on reconnaissance sorties.

Heavy anti-aircraft fire met reconnaissance aircraft over Syrian held territory on 3 December 1983. The United States launched a major strike the following day to remove the anti-aircraft batteries. Mutual assertions of self-defense, as in the cases of *GREER*, *MADDOX*, and *TURNER JOY*, again led the United States into open combat in "peacetime." In this case, two U.S. aircraft were lost, one naval officer was killed, and another

---

[58]"Key Sections of Pentagon's Report," A11:6 and A12:1.

was taken prisoner.[59]

At the President's news conference 2 weeks after the engagement he was asked about the status of the captured naval officer. The President answered, "The Syrians claim he's a prisoner of war when there is no declared war between nations. I don't think that makes you eligible for the Geneva Accords."[60] The answer indicates the changes in the legal situation were still not fully understood by the President at the end of December. How, then, could U.S. commanders on the scene understand their legal situation and its tactical implications? Moreover, even if the status of neutral and belligerent rights did remain in question, the 1949 Geneva Conventions, as has been explained, protect the victims of any scale of armed conflict (especially once it has an international character). Therefore, it was in the U.S. interest (or at least the interest of the U.S. naval officer held prisoner) to hold the Conventions applied in this case. By doing so Syria would be held responsible for compliance with the specific standards of treatment guaranteed by the Geneva Conventions regarding any U.S. prisoner they held or would hold.[61]

THE WAR POWERS RESOLUTION

When Congress repealed the Gulf of Tonkin Resolution in January 1971, they also began a process that resulted in the War Powers Resolution. This was characterized as an attempt to recover that body's constitutional power to declare war—but that power was never lost. In essence, if not by intent, Congress sought control over the President's role as Commander-in-Chief.[62]

---

[59]"Navy Jets Shot Down in Raids", *The Boston Globe*, 4 December 1983, 30:6 and Alan Cowell, "U.S. Warships Hit Syrian Positions in Lebanon Hills", *The New York Times*, 19 December 1983, A1:3.

[60]"President's News Conference on Foreign and Domestic Issues", *The New York Times*, 21 December 1983, A22:6. In a February 1994 conversation with an authoritative government source, this writer learned that Department of Defense lawyers were successful in getting the President to communicate a "clarification" of this statement to the Syrians.

[61]Schindler, 4n-5n, and Rubin, "Reagan's Error," A22:3-4.

[62]50 USC § 1541, 84 Stat. 2053-2055, Public Law 91-672, 12 Jan. 1970, Sec. 12; see also Whiteman, 12, 59.

The War Powers Resolution was passed over the veto of President Nixon in late 1973.[63] The intent was to limit the President's authority to place the United States in a situation identical to war by exercising his powers as Commander-in-Chief, and by-passing Congress, which is charged by the Constitution with responsibility for declaring war.[64]

There is no intention to explore the legal questions regarding "war powers" under Constitutional law in this work. The Act, however, does indirectly affect the question of the President espousing a U.S. policy claiming to be "neutral" whenever possible and is examined in that context.[65] In fact, the limitations imposed by the War Powers Resolution are more psychological than legal. The authority to order military action is vested in the President as Commander-in-Chief. If nothing else, the War Powers Resolution increases domestic pressure on the Commander-in-Chief to avoid acknowledging, for as long as possible, that hostilities could draw U.S. forces in the area into the conflict. To do so would engage the congressional position on war powers authority and the ensuing debate would limit policy options for coercive diplomacy and potentially erode the credibility of actions taken or threatened. The Act causes Executive Branch reluctance to acknowledge a U.S. departure from impartiality as quickly as belligerents might perceive it. If partiality increases the threat to naval forces, failure to recognize or acknowledge it only exacerbates the situation.

In 1979, President Carter moved an enormous naval force into the North Arabian Sea in response to the situations in U.S.

---

[63]Richard Nixon, "Veto of War Powers Resolution (Oct. 24, 1973)," *Department of State Bulletin* 69 , no. 1796 (1976), 662.

[64]"Pres Nixon Vetos War-Powers Bill Limiting Pres Powers to Commit Armed Forces to Foreign Hostilities Without Cong Approval", *The New York Times*, 25 October 1973, 1:8. "U.S. HR and Sen, on 7 Nov, Vote to Override Pres Nixon's Veto of War-Powers Bill, Which Curbs Pres Power to Commit U.S. Forces Abroad Without Cong Approval; HR Vote is 284-135, Only 4 Votes More Than Required 2/3; Sen Vote is 75-18, 13 More", *The New York Times*, 8 November 1973, 1:8.

[65]For an excellent discussion of the issues involved and the practice of Presidents since passage of the Act, see Robert D. Clark, et al., *The War Powers Resolution* (Washington, DC: National Defense University, 1985).

hostages crisis in Iran and the Soviet military intervention in Afghanistan's civil war to stabilize the recently installed Communist government there. Those U.S. forces were sustained in place for almost a decade, expanding and deploying further north into the Gulf of Oman, astride the Straits of Hormuz, and into the Persian Gulf as escorts for U.S. (and ultimately other) shipping when the Iran-Iraq war threatened to expand to trading partners and neighboring states. Though rarely characterized as such, these latter operations were in defense of U.S. and the international community's rights to the freedom of the sea and the freedom to use international waters by neutral vessels even in time of war.

In later events in the region in 1987 and 1988, reluctance to admit that hostile action against U.S. forces might be imminent (and trigger the provisions of the War Powers Act) apparently increased the danger to U.S. forces in the Persian Gulf. Admiral William J. Crowe, then Chairman, Joint Chiefs of Staff, told a Senate subcommittee:

> There were "a number of times last year" when "we considered doing things we thought would be wise to protect ourselves," but on advice from Defense Department lawyers the measures were not undertaken to avoid War Powers Resolution limitations.[66]

Congressional agreement or acquiescence had been obtained before the conduct of combat operations, without overtly engaging the provisions of the Act.

In *Desert Storm*, after obtaining authority for coalition forces to use all necessary means to support the collective self-defense

---

[66]Rick Maze, "War Powers Resolution Hindered Navy in Gulf, Crowe Tells Hill Panel", *Navy Times*, 3 October 1988, 29:1. It remains unclear from open source material exactly what these actions were. Reflection on the operations conducted there, however, gives the clear indication that selective responses against military targets such as armed oil platforms and others used as intelligence support facilities for Iranian maritime operations in the Gulf were on the list of options.

of Kuwait from the U.N. Security Council,[67] President Bush won a close vote in the Senate, with the House concurring, gaining domestic authority to act to enforce the Security Council decision.[68] The congressional votes constituted the legal equivalent of a declaration of war in support of the Security Council resolutions that had the character of an ultimatum for Iraq. The congressional action gave the President the moral benefit of a unified demonstration of national will in the hope Iraq would back down and withdraw from Kuwait. Equally important, the President was given the flexibility to act in a manner that did not jeopardize the safety of coalition forces. Pre-disclosure of the timing of the initial attack on Iraq's forces and command and control infrastructure might have diminished its phenomenal success and increased the extremely minimal casualties suffered.

But we must remember that domestic consensus is not always available. Even in the case of blatant Iraqi aggression against Kuwait it was narrowly achieved, even though military action could gain unprecedented consensus in the U.N. Security Council. It certainly damages morale, and possibly much deeper interests, when internal government disputes over the distribution of constitutional powers make the business of those sworn to defend the Constitution more dangerous.

OTHER CASES

•   In October 1973, President Nixon sent the carriers *JOHN F. KENNEDY, FRANKLIN D. ROOSEVELT,* and *INDEPENDENCE* as mobile airfields for the short-range aircraft used to rearm Israel after that country was shocked and severely hurt by the surprise Egyptian attack of 6 October. NATO allies of the United States, to preserve their neutrality, refused to allow

---

[67]UNSC Res. 678 of 29 November 1991. See also Peter David, *Triumph in the Desert* (New York: Random House, 1991), 58.

[68]David, 59. It is worth noting that this vote could not have been successfully obtained anytime between the Iraqi invasion of Kuwait on 2 August 1992 and the conclusion of the congressional elections in November of that year. Section 8 of the War Powers Resolution specifically excludes United Nations operations from its requirements.

U.S. cargo planes on rearming missions to land at bases in their territory (as Israel's defense is not included in the North Atlantic Treaty). During the airlift, an Egyptian destroyer fired on the U.S. merchant vessel *LA SALLE* in the Bab el Mandeb.[69]

•   In 1982 the Reagan Administration struggled to prevent an escalation of hostilities after an Argentine amphibious operation gained military control of the Falkland-Malvinas Islands. Partiality might have been a better public posture for the United States from the outset. The Argentines might well have been more disposed to negotiate a solution if they understood the United States would support British operations to regain control of the islands. When the Congress voted to support Great Britain and declared the United States "cannot stand neutral,"[70] partiality was no longer in question, no matter what the Reagan Administration had in mind. This congressional "decision" gave rise to accusations of perfidy from the Argentines who believed the United States had never been impartial, even when earlier offering its "good offices" to attempt a resolution of the conflict through diplomacy.[71]

•   Some states allow their animosity for the United States

---

[69]Elmo R. Zumwalt, *On Watch* (New York: Quadrangle, 1976), 442; Henry Kissinger, *Years of Upheaval* (Boston: Little, Brown & Co., 1982), 708-709. Also, "Only Portugal (which curiously formally declared its neutrality) and the Netherlands continued to allow supply of Israel (by the United States) from their territories. The general refusal to allow transit rights to the United States in its attempt to resupply the Israelis caused severe strains in the NATO alliance, and the Netherlands failure to conform to this decision similarly caused strains in the European Economic Community." Cable, *Gunboat*, 19-20; and Norton, 295-296; Norton also notes that the United States claimed neutrality through the Yom Kippur War despite the fact that such extraordinary efforts were taken to support Israel, 260.

[70]"Backing Britain on the Falklands -- What Next?", *U.S. News & World Report*, 10 May 1982, 27.

[71]A personal visit to the Argentine War College in May 1989 revealed that senior Argentine military personnel were still extremely bitter about the U.S. actions during the war. Another visit, in 1993, with their War College class and high ranking members of the Argentine Defense and Foreign Ministries and their legislature raised not one mention of the war policy of the United States— a marked change. The Menem Administration has clearly focused Argentine energies on the future instead of the past.

to erupt into violence even when they are not engaged in open combat with another belligerent. The experiences of *PUEBLO* and the Navy EC-121 were eruptions of the still simmering Korean War. The Gulf of Sidra incident, in which Libyan fighters were shot down after unsuccessfully attacking U.S. Navy carrier aircraft to assert their sovereignty over the waters of the Gulf, is another case involving competing rights and claims resulting in mutual self-defense.

• In June 1982, a Vietnamese vessel, without warning or apparent purpose, attacked two of three U.S. warships about 70 miles off the coast of Vietnam. The engagements were brief but the action lasted 8 hours. *TURNER JOY*, the victim of the Gulf of Tonkin incident in the same waters 18 years earlier, was slightly damaged during the initial firing when she approached the contact to identify it, but sustained no casualties. The vessel fired two red flares across *TURNER JOY*'s bow and immediately opened up with automatic weapons fire. Rounds penetrated the ship's side entering the wardroom. *LYNDE McCORMICK* was fired upon when she closed to assist and returned fire with her .50-calibre machine guns—but purposefully fired over the vessel. *BENJAMIN STODDART* was present but was not engaged. Neither she nor *LYNDE McCORMICK* was damaged in the action.

These incidents all demonstrate willingness by unfriendly states to use force against the United States, or more precisely, unsuspecting U.S. targets.[72] Nevertheless, in comparison to the first 25 years after World War II the post-Vietnam era was relatively calm until 1983.

---

[72]"U.S. Says That 2 Navy F-14 Jets Shot Down 2 Soviet-Built Libyan SU-22's About 60 Miles From Libyan Coast After Being Fired On by One of the Libyan Aircraft", *The New York Times*, 20 August 1981, 1:6. For the U.S. Navy analysis of the event see Dennis R. Neutze, "The Gulf of Sidra Incident: A Legal Perspective", *USNIP*, January 1982, 26-31. For the incident in the South China Sea see Richard Gross, "Warships Draw Fire", *Newport Daily News*, 23 June 1982, 12. See also Christopher C. Wright, "U.S. Naval Operations in 1982", *USNIP*, May 1983, 225.

7.
PERSPECTIVE

A State may be neutral, insofar as it does not participate in hostilities, even though it may not be impartial. Whether or not a successful position of nonparticipation is possible, in the absence of complete impartiality, is quite another question.[1]

HISTORICAL ASSESSMENT

Remember the *MAINE*!—that is, remember that no one can be sure if *MAINE* was actually attacked. And, if *MAINE* was attacked no one could prove it was Spain and not the Cuban insurgents who attacked her. We only know there was a predisposition to believe she was attacked and that decisionmakers at the time believed it enough to go to war. Further, consider the lingering doubts that continue to be raised about the Gulf of Tonkin incident. From these examples, the dangers of December 1971 should give us pause.

The entire Indo-Pakistani episode illustrates an ever-growing problem that will confront U.S. naval planners through the remainder of this century and beyond. The dangers of unneutral U.S. policy have been minimized to date by the preponderance of power behind the U.S. flag at sea. The objective or absolute measurement of U.S. power can be expected to retain its edge against likely adversaries; however, the subjective or relative power of the United States is less than only a decade ago. "Right-sizing" our forces is appropriate and an economic reality. This does not mean forces can do all the things they once could

---

[1]*NWIP 10-2*, 2-9n.

125

do simultaneously, nor does it mean they will be perceived the same way by coastal states empowered by what has been referred to as the military technological revolution with potent sea denial forces. The local relative combat power balance is shifting, and combined with perceived U.S. reluctance to act when the stakes in terms of likely combat losses are high in comparison to the benefits obtained through military action, will likely embolden coastal states as never before in this century.

Remember, the Monroe Doctrine was asserted against the European monarchies when our Navy was small and new by international standards. Young self-confident governments with small military forces can be quite adventurous. This problem is especially clear when the potential for problems is viewed situationally. U.S. forces operating close to troubled shores far from friendly bases could prove quite vulnerable in the given place and time.[2]

The foregoing analyses illustrating the inability of the United States to deal with the impartiality requirements of the law of neutrality is not a condemnation of U.S. policy. Neither is it an attempt to claim that naval forces are inappropriate for assigned missions. On the contrary, it clearly demonstrates the versatility and utility of naval forces even in exceptionally adverse circumstances. But why make those circumstances any more adverse than necessary? This historical review demonstrates there is good reason to examine more closely the legal consequences of otherwise useful policy to ensure that there are no hidden costs which would argue for a different course of action. Or, if the policy is affirmed by this legal examination, U.S. forces can then proceed to influence the execution of that policy better informed and thus less exposed to risk.

Remember, surprise is on everyone's list of the principles of war. Therefore, denying a potential enemy the advantage of surprise is part of effective preparation for action. It is clear, in light of the previous chapters, that a fuller understanding of the

---

[2]As Sir James Cable reflected, "In the last 37 years . . . it is hard to identify a significant dispute in which the factors of location, time, motivation, international environment and level of conflict were not, collectively or individually, more important than aggregate resources." Cable, *Gunboat*, 53.

law as it pertains to a naval commander's mission and situation will help reduce the enemy's element of surprise. Viewed this way, understanding these aspects of international law becomes a subset of the principles of war for naval commanders operating in the vicinity of belligerent forces or territory.

In the 20th century the United States became a world power, offering the country many advantages but also bringing many responsibilities the United States was slow to recognize and reluctant to accept. That reluctance was evidenced in rejection of League of Nations membership and the isolationism of the thirties. Since World War II and the advent of the United Nations the global interests of the United States have forced a more active participation in world affairs. This is all the more true in the post-Cold War world. In each case, U.S. participation reflects the best efforts of well-intentioned people with all the limitations human frailty bestows upon them. Frequently, the risks inherent in their policies are clear only with the benefit of hindsight.

A grasp of international law can help anticipate these problems because it provides an insight into the likely perspective of other nations. International law has not been developed arbitrarily: its substantive rules express the collective expectations and long-range interests of most nations in the case of customary law and incorporates all the variables that affect negotiations in the case of treaty law. These expectations, interests, and variables are also the essence of international relations. Action in excess of a state's authority, just like failure to use that authority in some situations, confuses allies and allows unnecessary advantages to antagonists. The law therefore provides a touchstone for objective policy evaluation outside of the subjective environment of national policy development.

It is not reasonable to expect that policy will always be perfectly conceived or executed. What is imperative, however, is that policy be developed as carefully as possible when lives and the fortune of the state are at stake. Further, domestic political considerations must be accepted as part of the strength of our political system but should refine policy formulation rather than detract from the effectiveness of national policy or increase the risks to those charged with its execution. That is, the facts of a situation cannot be changed by attaching domestically attractive labels.

If more candor will reduce diplomatic and military losses, more candor is required. If that candor will make the policy unacceptable domestically, the policy will eventually prove unacceptable anyway and should not be pursued. Attaching the correct legal labels will allow on-scene commanders greater understanding of the facts in dangerous situations.

THE FUTURE

Interdependence portends ever increasing demands on a country with expanding reliance on access to the world's resources. In 1982 the Department of Defense reported the United States was importing more than 50 percent of its needs for 21 different strategic materials. In half those cases the actual percentage of imports exceeded 90 percent. These statistics do not consider energy resources.[3] The broad and increasing economic interdependence of the United States may now lead, rather than reflect, our political interests.

The commitment to reconcile our national policy goals to an attainable consensus in the United Nations more frequently deepens our involvement with, support for, and responsiveness to, the expectations and aspirations of the international community in general.

A neutral United States put troops into Surinam in fall 1941 when the Dutch were at war with Germany. Access to the oil resources of Persian Gulf states today is a topic of continuing concern. *Desert Storm* confirmed that we will not tolerate access to those resources being in question. Willingness to threaten force to assure access to strategic or otherwise essential supplies is, in general, directly proportional to dependence upon external sources. This willingness also applies to the lines of communication along which these supplies must move. Disputes arising within or near the sources of these supplies will demand the attention of the United States. Impartiality regarding these

---

[3]U.S. Department of Defense, *Annual Report -- Department of Defense, Fiscal Year 1982* (Washington: GPO, 1981), 22.

disputes is not a likely U.S. response, at least not for long.

Coincident with the growth of interdependence, small states have acquired formidable sea denial forces. States that could previously be influenced by U.S. power now may choose another option. Besides purposeful actions, they can make the waters off their coasts exceptionally inhospitable by "accidental" engagements or unacknowledged surprise attacks and retain "plausible deniability." Such actions can unacceptably increase the costs of naval diplomacy.

An aircraft carrier could be damaged severely enough to temporarily lose its mission capability by actions such as a missile or suicide attack causing a flight deck or hangar fire. The same result could follow a collision at sea with a ship owned (or controlled) by a belligerent (or otherwise unfriendly state) but sailing under a flag of convenience. A collision could even result in the loss of a smaller ship. In short, the targets of U.S. suasion efforts have the option to raise the stakes of the game with relative impunity if they are determined enough. Such actions can be precipitated by U.S. policy decisions and statements by U.S. Government officials when viewed in light of the law of neutrality.

If today's naval officers are to recognize the difference between peacetime steaming and standing in "harm's way,"[4] they must fully understand not only U.S. policy, practice, and legal position, but equally comprehend a contending belligerent's interests, objectives, and priorities (which may prove infinitely more difficult to assess). This major challenge must be met by those who aspire to command. Their mission, and perhaps even the lives of those in their charge, may depend on it.

The technology of our age already militates strongly against self-sufficiency, thus driving the United States toward ever-increasing international economic entanglements with attendant political implications. Traditional interests and their implicit

---

[4]"I wish to have no connection with any ship which does not sail fast for I intend to go in harm's way". Attributed to John Paul Jones. The words are immortalized in his crypt under the U.S. Naval Academy Chapel. Surely the CO's of *PANAY*, *LIBERTY*, and *PUEBLO* were placed in harm's way even though their ships were not fast.

alliances will continue to commit the United States even in the absence of formal treaty relationships, as George Washington predicted. Consideration of national interests will present more significant impediments to impartiality.

The expansion and deepening of trade relationships may strengthen the peace with trading states but also tend to make peace indivisible where they are concerned. With or without treaties, threats to those states are, in essence, threats to the interests of the United States.

The role of law in situations that threaten the peace is often underestimated. Law is criticized for not accommodating the political and military realities of the present day world on the one hand, or because it demands states take actions that may lead to a rupture on the other. These criticisms may sometimes be valid. More often than not, though, the situation is best assessed by this observation from Professor Leo Gross: "Legal arguments aired by governments on suitable occasions may in fact be legal cloaks for political ends. What causes wars in such a situation is not the cloak but the clash of seemingly irreconcilable political ends."[5]

The exigencies of world politics do not yet preclude neutrality, but they do prevent great powers from maintaining that status most of the time. Widely read international relations pundits such as Palmer and Perkins remind us that, "As the 'realists' like to emphasize, this is a great power world, and the major decisions in world affairs, including the ultimate decisions on war or peace, are being and will continue to be made by the most powerful states."[6]

When power is used to influence the conduct of world affairs it gives rise to a responsibility among states to ensure that those affairs are not influenced officiously or unjustly. Officious action, meddling in affairs legally beyond the concern of the actor, makes enemies of even one's friends, or makes tools of them and destroys their own constituency bases. Failure to defend one's proper legal interests, on the other hand, also undermines alliances and breeds domestic disillusion.

---

[5]Gross, "States as Organs of International Law," 85.

[6]Norman D. Palmer and Howard C. Perkins, *International Relations*, 3rd ed. (Boston: Houghton Mifflin, 1969), 713.

Perceptions of justice in the various power centers will, unfortunately, differ. Nevertheless, each must do its best to preserve justice without threatening the peace. When a choice must be made between peace and justice, choosing peace does not always strengthen that peace and may have the opposite effect in the long run.

THE ROLE OF NAVAL DIPLOMACY

The imperfections of this world will not soon be eliminated, so decisionmakers must be careful to employ their foreign policy tools responsibly. This is a moral imperative because while "there is such a thing as *Raison d'Etat*. . . . On occasions it spills blood."[7]

The policy of acting in support of a set of principles considered conducive to world peace is a good start. These principles must include a commitment to preserving justice as well as peace. The Charter of the United Nations articulates a set of principles that reflect the collective values of its framers. It was also accepted as legally binding by the United States. The bottom line of the system established therein is that force may be appropriate when justice is at stake, and force is always permitted for self-defense under Article 51.

The "justice" of an armed conflict is to be determined by whoever is chosen by the parties to a dispute to help mediate, arbitrate, or adjudicate their disagreement (under the peaceful settlement procedures of Article 33 of the Charter). Or, the Security Council can define justice and impose a solution as a political decision under Article 39.[8] The legality of an individual

---

[7]Richard K. Smith, "The Violation of the *LIBERTY*", *USNIP*, June 1978, 70.

[8]The Charter of the United Nations, Article 33 (1), provides: "The parties to any dispute, the continuation of which is likely to endanger the maintenance of international peace and security, shall, first of all, seek a solution by negotiation, enquiry, mediation, conciliation, arbitration, judicial settlement, resort to regional agencies or arrangements, or other peaceful means of their choice. Article 39 provides: "The Security Council shall determine the existence of any threat to the peace, breach of the peace, or act of aggression and shall make recommendations, or decide what measures shall be taken . . . to maintain or restore international peace and security."

state's subjective political assessment of "justice" also can be determined through a decision by the International Court of Justice, which is binding on parties to a case under Article 94 (1) of the Charter.[9]

To avoid conflicts pitting the great powers against one another, the United Nations cannot legally decide to take action which a Permanent Member of the Security Council votes against. This means that in some cases the "veto" of a Permanent Member can frustrate the political process of Article 39 by preventing a decision regarding which side to a dispute is just and what action should be taken to resolve the dispute. Or, a Permanent Member could prevent the Security Council from deciding on enforcement measures, expected under Article 94 (2) of the Charter,[10] to uphold the legal decisions of the International Court of Justice. In effect, differing views of "justice" can frustrate the positive law.

All that can be expected in such situations is that states act in a manner consistent with the basic principles of the Charter. Barring a qualified majority consensus in the Security Council, states are free to decide the justice of the situation for themselves. They can then take action in varying degrees in collective self defense of one side or the other—or declare themselves neutral. Whether there should there be another option is discussed in chapter 8.

Applying this philosophy of acting in accordance with the principles of the Charter to decisions regarding U.S. naval diplomacy operations can best be done by committing naval forces to situations where "rights" can be cited as well as "interests." The right of self-defense guaranteed by Article 51 is quite broad but there is a qualitative difference between defending what is legally seen as a right and what is asserted as

---

[9]The Charter of the United Nations, Article 94 (1) provides: "Each Member of the United Nations undertakes to comply with the decision of the International Court of Justice in any case to which it is a party."

[10]The Charter of the United Nations, Article 94 (2), provides: "If any party to a case fails to perform the obligations incumbent upon it under a judgment rendered by the Court, the other party may have recourse to the Security Council, which may, if it deems necessary, make recommendations or decide upon measures to be taken to give effect to the judgment."

an interest. Using power to influence or coerce where only interests justify the action will weaken the peace by providing precedents that can be cited with political effect by states with hegemonic or other narrow policy motivations. U.S. actions that might justify others so motivated cannot be part of a pursuit of justice in the international community.

Although it is frequently possible to have competing rights, those situations sometimes can be understood and resolved in terms of competing priorities. They lend themselves more readily to the methods of peaceful settlement. When the issues in conflict involve interests alone, and they have come to the point where the peace is threatened, while the law might address issues such as economic need and equity, reality will tend toward political clout and "might makes right" types of resolutions which undermine international stability in the long run.

Even when action is considered expedient to force a quick just solution to a dispute, if "rights" are not involved, "justice" becomes highly subjective, and the action may do more harm than good in terms of the precedents set. Power used where persuasion and diplomacy could accomplish the same ends is power abused. And, as Professor Rubin explains:

> Ignoring the weapons that traditions of law place at the disposal of United States negotiators to further United States interests in "political" disputes does not simplify the world, it complicates it, and United States economic interests in stability and peace suffer as well as United States political and military interests.[11]

Beyond more awareness of the legal situation, which in no way prevents behavior in accordance with firmly held values and priorities, the facts of the situation must be plainly addressed. When the United States, in responding to its values and priorities, finds that it must abandon impartiality, the intention to defend the right to do so should be openly stated. This removal of ambiguity regarding intentions will increase the deterrent effect

---

[11]Alfred P. Rubin, "The Panama Canal Treaties: Locks on the Barn Door", *The Year Book of World Affairs*, 1981, 192.

of U.S. power. It will also alert U.S. military forces to the danger of that deterrence failing and suddenly openly involving them in armed conflict, perhaps at the initiative of the other side.

Talk of peace and neutrality and orders stressing the importance of a legal status already abandoned or compromised can deceive responsible military leaders about the imminence of the threat they face instead of focusing them on the increased need for a vigilant defensive posture. *DOLPHIN*'s small boat, *PANAY*, Pearl Harbor's battleship row, *LIBERTY*, *PUEBLO*, the ill-fated EC-121, the sailors and Marines lost in Beirut, and many others are foreboding reminders of the costs.

When such risks are understood, chances improve for minimizing losses. Vietnamese motor torpedo boats sunk in the Gulf of Tonkin and Libyan gunboats and fighters at the bottom of the Gulf of Sidra bear witness to that. Commanders in those incidents did not surrender the advantage of surprise to the enemy. Awareness of the threat was recognized in a timely manner, thus preventing unnecessary American losses.

DOES THE LAW FOSTER PEACE WITH JUSTICE?

If a purpose of law in war is to help attain a better peace than existed before its outbreak, then law that regulates war should be framed to control the scope of the conflict. Law that precipitates unnecessary escalation moves the war further from the peace and makes its restoration more difficult. Such law would then defeat its own purpose, and it would not be good law.

Good law must consider practice and regulate that practice as feasible. Infeasible controls lead inevitably to violations that, in turn, lead to broadening of the conflict and a lack of respect for law.

The law of neutrality is intended to protect states from the effect of wars they can afford to avoid or cannot afford to join; impartiality does not always provide the best path to that end. This fact is given tacit recognition by the neutrality regimes of the Suez and Panama Canals. The canals are open to the ships of belligerents equally, and the use of the waterways by belligerent ships is not considered a violation of the neutrality of

Egypt or Panama as other uses of their territory would.[12] Likewise, neutral states are required not to close international straits within their territorial seas in time of war. Waters within the territory of the neutral state remain as accessible to belligerents as the high seas for the purpose of transit.

These examples can be seen as granting a primacy for the concept of freedom of the seas over neutral duties. Or, they can be seen as an acknowledgement of something more pragmatic. A neutral trying to deny a belligerent access to international waters even though it passes through its territorial sea might soon find the belligerent conducting an operation to ensure its ability to use those waters, if such action were at all within its power. This would broaden the combat and bring the neutral into the fighting.

So the law of neutrality provides limits validated by history and guidance for behavior based on pragmatic policy concerns of all states. But the law of neutrality may not accommodate clearly—as yet—the reality of the world the United States must deal with without great risks.

Recognizing this situation, it follows that if a power finds itself in situations that prevent full impartiality, but still desires to avoid participation in the war, good law would not only permit but would protect that option where it was also seen as in the

---

[12]Previously the Panama Canal was neutral only as long as the United States was neutral. Since the United States ratified the Panama Canal Treaties, TIAS 10029, 10030, 10031, 10032, 10039, 10043, 10044, 10045, 10046, and 10061, the neutrality regime for the canal matches that used for the Suez Canal in the Treaty of Constantinople of 1888. That treaty kept the British controlled Suez Canal open to Russian warships during the Russo-Japanese War even though Japan was an ally of Britain. It was also open to Italian warships during the invasion of Ethiopia in the face of League of Nations efforts (including the British) to stop Italy's aggression. The rationale behind this permanent neutrality is to have the canals be seen as benefits by belligerents, not as targets. If a belligerent cannot safely transit to or from these canals, however, guaranteed access is of little value. Hopefully such disenfranchised belligerents will also lack the ability to attack the canals. See John Noel Petrie, *Potential Problems for U.S. Naval Policy Evidenced in International Law* a Doctoral Thesis submitted to the Faculty of the Fletcher School of Law and Diplomacy, May 1990, 154-236 (also available from UMI) for an analysis of this and others legal and naval policy questions raised by the new treaties.

interest of all states.

The question remains, can the law that has survived so long in the face of such violent conflicts be amended by the consent of the states it serves and who enforce it? And, would such a modification remove problems or merely change the problem set?

8.
PRESCRIPTION

*While the peacetime presence and crisis response components
of our Maritime Strategy are less detailed and formal than the
warfighting component, they are no less important.*[1]

SUMMARY

Situation

What has been widely referred to as the presence mission likely
will continue to see broad use in the era of the "From the Sea"
strategy. Operations in support of United Nations decisions will
likewise find the U.S. Navy off the coasts of nations close to—or
embroiled in—war. The legal environment and the relative
power equation must be understood both from our own
perspective and that of any potential adversary.

Further, it must be recognized that inexperienced officers in
charge of shore batteries, missile patrol boats, submarines, and
coastal state aircraft do not necessarily have a world view of the
situation; they may not be able to easily recognize important
distinctions between rhetoric and reality. The allure of becoming
a national hero for successfully engaging one vulnerable unit
from what their political leaders' rhetoric has labeled an "enemy"
nation could well mask the risk of plunging their state into a
disasterous war.

Preponderant U.S. power is no longer always the rule. The
available U.S. naval forces are coming into closer balance with

---

[1]Admiral James D. Watkins, U.S. Navy, Chief of Naval Operations, "The
Maritime Strategy," in United States Naval Institute, *The Maritime Strategy*
(Annapolis: Naval Institute Press, January 1986), 5.

their potential adversaries, at least at the scene of action. Policy makers must heed the warning of Hermocrates:

> Many before have set out to punish aggression, and many others also have been confident that their power would secure them some advantage. Of these, the former, so far from being revenged, have often been destroyed, and with the latter it has often happened that . . . they have had to give up what they had already.[2]

This work reviews a number of previous operations in light of the law of neutrality and its underpinning logic and takes a longer view than might have been possible at the time the operations were conducted. The "lessons learned" included that the belligerent nation's view of U.S. actions regarding the law of neutrality might provide an insight into the risks involved. Also, a consistent pattern of less than impartial conduct when operating near other nations' wars indicates that this practice will continue throughout the future. That is, the legal environment was studied so that its benefits and hazards could be understood. The law can be an important factor in decisions regarding naval forces. This examination has identified some problems and, so far, implied some solutions. This final chapter summarizes these issues and adds some as well.

Responsibilities of Planners

Naval planning is done in the most conscientious manner possible. This appears a large assumption to make, but it remains an appropriate one, because those who do the naval planning understand that they are responsible for good stewardship of the national resources in their charge. Further, they are accountable to many who will, albeit indirectly, oversee naval planning and its results. These overseers expect to receive thoroughness and care from the naval planner.

The taxpayers expect their naval forces to assume risks in the

---

[2]Thucydides, *History of the Pelopennesian War*, trans. Rex Warner with Introduction and Notes by M.I. Finley (Baltimore: Penguin Books, 1972), Book IV, chap. 4, para. 62, 301.

interest of national policy. They also expect the national treasure invested in the physical plants and combat systems of the warships to be husbanded carefully. And the sailors themselves must be given the clearest possible assessment of the situation they stand into and concise direction to achieve attainable objectives. Finally, the sailors' families are entitled to have every possible member of our Armed Forces return home safe and sound.

Support to the Naval Force Commander

It is impossible to tell from reading the history of a series of events whether or not the implications of the law were originally considered by those who made or influenced naval policy. Surely it was a factor in at least some of the situations. The pragmatic logic that created the law likely played a role in almost all of them.

Law is already considered in the planning of naval operations. The situations examined, however, indicate that the law can have a definite role for those making decisions at the scene of action at sea as well.

The naval force commander, be his force a single ship or a battle group, receives support and guidance for his operations from higher authority. The assigned operations and specific missions are framed for him in a number of ways, usually a Letter of Instruction (LOI), an Operations Order, an Alert Order, or, in extreme cases, in Execute Orders. Each of these documents explains the situation in which the force will operate, assigns specific missions, and when necessary, delineates appropriate rules of engagement.

That support and guidance may well consider every aspect of the law appropriate to the situation, but it does not articulate the law considered. Further, it may take a narrow view of the law, measuring the proposed operations against the United States' assertion or understanding of the legal situation. It is just as appropriate to include an assessment of the potential for an adversary to take action based on his interpretation of the legal situation as it is to provide an intelligence analysis of that adversary's purely political, ideological, or even religious motivations to take action. Presumably any action an adversary might take is the result of a policy decision on his part as well.

If the description of international law in chapter 1 holds true, the potential enemy's decisions should consider (either overtly or through subtle influence) international law as well. The adversary's rules of engagement, whether clearly articulated or not, likely consider specific criteria as prerequisites to act—whether that decision is ultimately made at high levels or locally. It is impossible to control for poor judgment on the part of an adversary; this is especially true when the adversary's on-scene commander is inexperienced and operating in an emotionally charged environment. Close attention to his leaders' rhetoric can indicate when this on-scene commander is likely to be confused about his nation's policy decisions or interpretations of the legal situation.

If the U.S. naval force commander were alerted to any legal tripwires inherent in his mission, it could improve the responsiveness of his force. As has been discussed, some U.S. policy decisions can help fulfill the requirements of a potential enemy's rules of engagement. If some U.S. action or pronouncement can cause an adversary to consider U.S. forces to be hostile, or allow otherwise routine operations to be perceived as demonstrating hostile intent, the U.S. commander needs to recognize the dangers of that situation, and checking the situation against the law can help.

Therefore, inclusion of a specific section addressing these legal issues in the standard format for each of the documents—such as LOIs or Operations Orders—that provides guidance to naval force or unit commanders should provide a number of benefits at no real cost. For example, it could:

• Assure that the higher authority consciously decided whether including a legal assessment was appropriate for the mission being assigned

• Provide a cross reference and separate scale for potential risk analysis aside from the overall intelligence assessment

• Give a more complete understanding of the local situation

• Enhance the utility of the rules of engagement by helping the naval force commander better anticipate the need to consult or execute them.

Most importantly, providing the legal assessment of the

situation would provide an opportunity to review the law from the potential adversary's perspective. This simple process would make the distinction, where necessary, between the U.S. policy and any other applicable interpretation of the law. This can have major implications when the United States is referring to itself publicly and privately as neutral because its policy is to avoid committing forces to the conflict as a belligerent—but technically unneutral actions have occurred removing the protections of strict neutrality, or when the law asserted by the United States is not understood the same way by the potential adversary. This need not be limited to the current concerns regarding neutrality. It would be equally useful in dealing with competing claims regarding maritime territory, maritime areas of jurisdiction, and questions involving the freedom of the sea.

One point of clarification on the need for including this legal analysis: the naval officer is reasonably well versed—or becomes so—regarding the law of war as it affects his authority to employ deadly force in pursuit of his military objectives. Further, the rules of engagement generally clarify these requirements and act as a double check to align his interpretation with that of his seniors. The law of neutrality, however, can be something of a stranger to the unrestricted line officer. Perhaps this is because of the way in which policy decisions are anticipated by the law. The political assumptions underlying the law of neutrality are not the standard fare of the warfare specialists who command forces at sea. And so, subtle departures from impartiality—which sometimes occur at great distance from the scene of action, or arise from differing perceptions of the situation and the law, or what constitutes self-defense rather than direct support to a belligerent—can cause problems.

The United States should use its naval forces to support U.S. policy wherever appropriate, but the level of that involvement should, whenever possible, be the result of a policy decision—not of miscalculation of the adversary's intentions. A legal analysis might improve the results of this effort. Removing the law from decisionmaking not only invites mistakes in policy, it is a mistake in policy.

Change in U.S. Practice (or Articulation)

Decisions regarding U.S. naval operations in which the use or threat of force can be anticipated are best made when we are committing naval forces to situations where "rights" can be cited as well as "interests." Given that the right of collective self-defense is not limited by, or to, treaty relationships, there should be few situations where examination of the fundamental reasons for U.S. involvement would not involve defense or exercise of legal rights. It should be publicly explained as such.

Should the Law be Changed?

Changing law, not an easy process, is generally accomplished in two ways: state practice that develops into customary law, or negotiated agreements expressed in treaty law. Both methods helped develop the current law that regulates the behavior of belligerent and neutral states. Because practical considerations argue against purposefully changing the law of neutrality solely through state practice (because this assumes the existence of armed conflict), updating the related treaties through agreement at an international conference is the most appropriate method. The international conference regarding the law of war at sea, proposed by Elmar Rauch, might provide the appropriate vehicle for this effort.[3] Consideration of whether the law should be changed proceeds within this context.

---

[3]Elmar Rauch points out that "There exists a gap between the development of the law of armed conflict and the law of the sea which cannot be bridged by way of interpretation or analogy." Rauch goes on to conclude, "We are desperately in need of such a codification conference, which might best be called 'the United Nations Conference on the Law of Armed Conflict at Sea'." See Elmar Rauch, "The Protocol Additional to the Geneva Conventions for the Protection of Victims of International Armed Conflicts and the United Nations Convention on the Law of the Sea: Repercussions on the Law of Naval Warfare." *Report to the Committee for the Protection of Human Life in Armed Conflict of the International Society for Military Law and the Law of War*, Bonn, Federal Republic of Germany, July 1983, 14-15 and 145. Conversation with Professor Rubin reveals that such an effort has been considered by the International Committee of the Red Cross.

It is worth noting that the Security Council could define precise rules for any specific situation when the situation requires a decision for enforcement. Such an innovation, though consistent with Charter law, would also need to be fully consistent with the practical aspects of the situation to be persuasive and effective. Further, the influence of such a decision likely would be *sui generis*.

On the other hand, some, including Kelsen, have argued that the neutrality that survived World War II was not necessarily impartial. The influence of the Charter principles and the experience of the war were thought to establish a new regime of law. Unneutral acts would not terminate the neutral status of a state. Only entry into the conflict through a policy decision evidenced in a declaration or consistent actions of the neutral or one of the belligerents (against the neutral) could terminate the state's status as a neutral.[4] Obviously this interpretation is not much different than the neutrality of the United States before World War II, when a neutral could not expect its partiality to be tolerated by the injured belligerent unless the belligerent took pause in consideration of the consequences of taking action against the neutral. (This is actually part of international law's "automatic enforcement," so to speak).

The intensity of the conflict and the relative power equation of the respective parties determine what policy the belligerent follows and how far the neutral may stray from impartiality without eliciting a reprisal or other reaction. The aggrieved belligerent may deal with the unneutral behavior through localized military, diplomatic, economic, legal, and other measures having major political effects regardless of the relative military, economic, and even political power situation in

---

[4]Kelsen, 156, 158; Tucker, 183, 197, 259; "The status of neutrality is terminated only when a neutral State resorts to war against a belligerent or when a belligerent resorts to war against a neutral." *NWIP 10-2*, para. 231; "Within great powers public opinion, affected by interested propaganda, sentimental preferences, juridicial ideas, and balance of power considerations, usually rapidly became unneutral and help short of war was given to the favored belligerent, often eventuating in war itself." Wright, 139.

isolation. In discussing various proposals to improve the International Court of Justice, Professor Leo Gross concluded, "More imaginative innovations may be needed to take into account the unprecedented interdependence of states in their international relations."[5] If this is an appropriate prescription for the Court, surely it is essential to the law itself as well.

The current law of neutrality is based on centuries of practice and agreements hammered out by negotiators in 1907 and confirmed in 1928 about what should not be accepted by belligerents. This law was developed when only power and pragmatism could argue to modify the law evidenced by the "practice-of-states-observed-until-then." Unfortunately, the practice has changed little. That is, Articles 2 and 33 of the U.N. Charter remain rules "for" rather than rules "of" international behavior.

Because a new treaty could appropriately include prescription for the future, perhaps another look at the law is warranted. With unpredictable dangers to the escalation of any conflict the restraint on expansion of war should be greater than was contemplated in 1907 and 1928. To the degree that the rules of law, such as the United Nations Charter, are an expression of the collective expectations of the states of the world, there is evidence that those same states expect a degree of partiality to be appropriate at times. Perhaps it is time to try to define what partial actions neutrals should be allowed to take and what actions belligerents should not tolerate. Or, maybe that would prove entirely situational. If a list of these actions could be developed, it would be useful to policy makers and commanders whether it could be made law or not, though clearly its influence would be magnified by codification.

The onset of World War II witnessed a metamorphosis of sorts in the terminology of wartime roles as viewed by the law. Instead of dealing in terms of neutral and belligerent states, the world was presented with a new articulation of status vis-à-vis

---

[5]Leo Gross, "The International Court of Justice: Considerations for Requirements for Enhancing Its Role in the International Legal Order," in Leo Gross, ed., *The Future of the International Court of Justice* (Dobbs Ferry, New York: Oceana, 1976), 1:36.

the conflict—non-belligerency. Just exactly what non-belligerency is seems to be defined only to the satisfaction of the states which consider themselves non-belligerent.

Although non-belligerence was most recently espoused in the late 1930s and early 1940s, committing unneutral acts through partiality has long been understood as within the law of neutrality. Grotius advocated it as a policy to favor a just cause. Today unneutral actions are simply a departure from the law of neutrality. In many cases such a departure is much more likely to result in limited reprisal by the aggrieved belligerent than in war, and the benefit to the favored belligerent may be evaluated as justifying the risks of reprisal or even war. In any case, international law is not a criminal law system with objective evaluations and community enforcement by direct action; it is a tort law system, where the reaction of the victim of a "wrong" is key to understanding what the law really is understood to be by the victim. State practice and the summary of declarations (below) include a number of cases in which states have been neither openly belligerent nor impartial.

There has been a growing tendency in this century both to avoid war and to pursue what is perceived as "justice" in international relations. The law of neutrality, if it includes impartiality, reduces the decision to act in support of a "just" belligerent to a question of choosing between peace and justice in many instances. Of course, states may reject impartiality without committing themselves to open fighting, but they do so without the protection of the traditional law of neutrality, or at least without its unambiguous protection.

If the law recognized non-belligerence as a legal status it is possible belligerent states would take greater pause in making the policy decision whether a reprisal is the appropriate response to specific unneutral conduct or if some less stringent protest might be more appropriate. If a state gained some flexibility under the law of neutrality to act, without forfeit of its protections, in support of a belligerent deemed by a broad consensus to be acting on just cause—and this new interpretation were supported by a collective security alliance or coalition, the law might actually be strengthened. Justice might be better served if states contemplating belligerent reprisal would have to consider that they would be confronting more than the military power of the so-called non-belligerent.

The industrial and economic strength of states could be better brought to bear in a crisis. States participating in the broad consensus, while unable or unwilling to take a military role, might take limited action by forgoing their own impartiality to impose sanctions to help enforce the consensus view of "justice" if this proposed new law extended protections such as those which currently exist for neutrals to the self-declared non-belligerent. This would bring into the laws of war and neutrality a protected status for states to fulfill their obligations under collective self-defense arrangements (formal or informal) short of joining the war as a belligerent (which many are reluctant to do anyway).

This is not inconsistent with the requirements of the United Nations Charter prior to or absent action by the Security Council. In fact, it is consistent with the situation that ensues when the Security Council decides on enforcement action. Under Article 25, states are obliged to comply with Security Council decisions but are not necessarily always obliged to engage the state being enforced against with combat forces.

This was the case when the coalition acted under Security Council Resolution 678 in collective self-defense of Kuwait while states not members of the coalition were obliged to comply with previously imposed sanctions including the embargo. This did not prevent Iran and Jordan from declaring neutrality.

This could then be seen as a contemporary, and legally accepted, example of United Nations authorized enforcement action permitting some states to be belligerents and expecting all other states to be non-belligerent (or at least not impartial) and allowing some states to be neutral. It is also consistent with other state practice in this century, and not only the practice of the United States as related earlier. Consider the following examples:

• During World War I, coincident with the U.S. declaration of war in 1917, the complexities of the world situation were leading other nations to shift from positions of neutrality to something else, but not all became formal belligerents.

Brazil, at the onset of hostilities in Europe, declared

neutrality (4 August 1914) but gradually found neutrality untenable. Brazil's path to belligerency was not direct.

> There was . . . a period under neutrality regulations . . . during . . . which . . . diplomatic relations with Germany were severed. This period (11 April to 11 June 1917) was followed by a period during which diplomatic relations were still severed and neutrality revoked and a recognition of the American "continental solidarity" was announced and spirit of friendship for the United States (a belligerent since April) was expressed without a declaration of war till October 26, 1917.[6]

• After the U.S. declared war, Costa Rica offered in April 1917 "the use of its waters and ports for war needs by the American Navy."[7] Peru opened ports to U.S. warships calling the action "benevolent neutrality."[8] El Salvador claimed to be "associated with the United States"[9] after the United States declared war. Uruguay, in June of 1917, proclaimed: " . . . no American country which in defense of its own rights should find itself in a state of war with nations of other continents will be treated as belligerents (sic)."[10]

Judge Jessup asserted:

> A basic assumption is that peace with justice is a desideratum.

---

[6]George Grafton Wilson, *ILS* XXXIV (1934), 70.

[7]George Grafton Wilson, ed., *ILS* XVII (1917), 77, "Note from the Government of Costa Rica, dated 12 April 1917."

[8]Ibid., 77, "Proclamation by M. Pardo, President of Peru, on 28 July 1917," 197-198.

[9]Ibid., "Salvador: Attitude on the War Between the United States and Germany, October 6, 1917," 210.

[10]Ibid., "Uruguay: Decree modifying neutrality regulations in case of war by American countries, June 18, 1917" from *U.S. Official Bulletin No. 35*, 2, at 249; 1907 Hague XIII, the "Convention Concerning the Rights and Duties of Neutral Powers in Naval War", II Malloy 2352-2366, Schindler and Toman, 855-864, to which none of these states became parties, but the United States and Germany had, holds in Article 5, "Belligerents are forbidden to use neutral ports and waters as a base of operations against their adversaries."

> The obstacles in the way of attaining such a peace are many.
> We should be sure that we do not increase the number of
> obstacles by a rigid adherence to traditional concepts which
> may have been the product of historical situations which do
> not have their counterpart today.[11]

The situation goes beyond being illogical—it is so ambiguous as to be dangerous. Since most armed conflict is of limited scope and duration it is frequently difficult to determine whether a war has begun in earnest or if what seems to be "war" is merely a series of isolated actions. The third state, whether partial to one side or not, might well have trade relations that aid either potential belligerent and are essential to the third state's economic interests. These trading rights might need to be defended by the neutral third state, while a disadvantaged belligerent might consider the associated transport to be subject to seizure or destruction.

While it seems clear that the law of war applies to all forms of hostilities between belligerents or parties engaged in the incidents within the context of the *jus in bello*, questions remain regarding when the law of neutrality becomes operative. For instance, when is a state acting in self-defense entitled to expect third states to prevent the use of areas under their jurisdiction by the opposing side? And, what degree of jurisdiction must the third state enjoy before the rights and obligations of the neutral apply (e.g., how does neutrality operate in an Exclusive Economic Zone, over a state's continental shelf, in archipelagic waters)? What are the prerequisites that, once completed, give rise to a right to act in reprisal against perceived unneutral acts?

The answers to these questions will always come down to unfettered auto-interpretation of the situation and the law: simply a policy decision—albeit a difficult one—by the state involved. Nothing can change that, but a treaty reflecting law that helped clarify these issues would become a factor in the decisionmaking process and might influence the results of these auto-interpretations in a helpful manner.

---

[11]Philip C. Jessup, "Should International Law Recognize an Intermediate Status Between Peace and War?" *AJIL* 48 (1954), 102-103.

The factual existence of stages between neutrality and belligerency or between peace and war is irrefutable. This provides the element of "the practice of states" to the law-making process. As yet it has not been persuasive in changing the law.

In legal terminology, that practice does not as yet include *opinio juris*: states do not behave that way because they believe the law requires it—they behave that way because they believe their policy priorities require it, hence customary law regarding non-belligerency as a separate status is not yet developed, nor is it in the process of developing. No amount of state practice can result in new customary law unless those states believe their practice to be required by the law as they understand it.

The existence of the status of non-belligerent is acknowledged in the Geneva Convention Relative to the Treatment of Prisoners of War regarding the obligation to intern members of the armed forces of the belligerents found in their territory. While this by no means defines the duties and obligations of non-belligerents in war it does limit their flexibility. It prevents a state from claiming to be non-belligerent and allowing its territory to be used as a base by one of the warring parties.[12]

---

[12]Geneva Convention Relative to the Treatment of Prisoners of War, signed 12 August 1949, (Convention III), TIAS 3364, UST 6, Article 4 B (2) states, "The persons belonging to one of the categories enumerated in the present Article, who have been received by neutral or non-belligerent Powers on their territory and whom these Powers are required to intern under international law, without prejudice to any more favorable treatment which these Powers may choose to give and with the exception of Articles 8, 10, 15, 30 fifth paragraph, 58-67, 92, 126 and, where diplomatic relations exist between the Parties to the conflict and the neutral or non-belligerent Power concerned, those Articles concerning the Protecting Power. Where such diplomatic relations exist the Parties to a conflict on whom these persons depend shall be allowed to perform towards them the functions of a Protecting Power as provided in the present Convention, within conformity with diplomatic and consular usage and treaties." (emphasis added); Schindler and Toman, 355-425; see also Whiteman, 11, 164. It is interesting to note that the International Committee of the Red Cross (ICRC) *Commentary* which examines the Geneva Conventions Article by Article discusses

If a more precisely defined status were to be agreed for the non-belligerent, it might permit states to give up certain neutral rights in exchange for specifically approved types of actions departing from impartiality while allowing them to remain immune from direct military action as belligerent reprisal. Perhaps humanitarian deliveries should be permitted specifically in the law rather than on a case-by-case basis, even when a port is blockaded or a town is besieged, for example.

Good law should reflect what is consistently accepted as good policy. The reality of global interdependence argues for this type of an exception to prevent threats to neutral or non-belligerent trade from causing a state to incur irreparable economic harm from a war in which it desires to remain "non-belligerent"—or, conversely, to prevent states from being drawn into a conflict for no reason other than to sustain an essential trade relationship with one of the belligerents.

Were such an accommodation to be made it would permit a state to add its strength (in part) to one side in an armed conflict in a manner that might cause the other belligerent to sue for peace or accept an armistice or cease-fire sooner, or on terms less favorable to itself than if all non-participants in the fighting had adhered to strict impartial neutrality. While this would not prevent a policy decision to engage the shipping of the non-belligerent state, if clear legal (and associated strategic) consequences flowed from such a decision, it might prove harder to make. That is, if doing so was not legally acceptable as a reprisal—which is a one-time punitive response—then an aggressor state would have to enlarge the list of enemies it was confronting for the duration of the conflict. The weight of the policy decision involved would be greater.

The very potential for third states to declare non-belligerence and still enjoy some protection under the law would provide would-be aggressors with reason for hesitation. Of course, this

---

only neutral states making no reference whatsoever to non-belligerents. See Jean S. Pictet, ed., *Commentary: I Geneva Convention for the Amelioration of the Conditions of the Wounded and Sick in Armed Forces in the Field* (Geneva: International Committee of the Red Cross, 1952).

could also give pause to the allies of the defending state, but could slow the escalation of any conflict by formalizing a step in collective self-defense. Non-belligerence would allow actions that do not broaden the conflict by committing additional forces to combat, yet put the aggressor on notice that allies and other non-belligerent supporters are prepared to make the aggressor's military objectives more difficult to attain.

The purpose of the law of war is to end war as quickly as possible with a minimum of suffering in an environment conducive to a lasting peace. In times past, perhaps only neutral and belligerent statuses were required to achieve those ends. Today those might be inadequate.[13]

If the current trend toward more frequent resort-to-the-authority for enforcement action under the Charter continues, non-belligerence might be required as a status if Security Council decisions are to have irresistible force.

Additionally, non-belligerence could present the opportunity for great powers to withhold their full force of arms from a conflict while still acting in behalf of their national interests. If the great powers successfully resist entering into open hostilities the potential for catastrophic escalation would be more easily averted; if they fail, they would at least have slowed the momentum of the conflict permitting a greater opportunity for its control.

---

[13]Cf. "Changing conditions require changing rules and . . . a law or peace and law of war dichotomy is inadequate in . . . contemporary situations." William O. Miller, "Belligerency and Limited War", *NWCR*, January 1969, 25. In the same vein: "The existence of a state of 'war,' in contrast to a state of 'peace,' has had a determinative effect upon the prescriptions regarded as applicable to events upon the sea. During 'peace' one set of laws has been regarded as relevant, and during 'war' an entirely different set of laws has been involved. It is no longer new, however, to suggest that this supposedly dichotomous state of affairs does not accurately depict the many nuances of contemporary state practice, and that 'peace' and 'war' are but the polar terms for the extremes of a continuum in exercise of coercion, not necessarily representing the only policy-relevant stages in that continuum." McDougal and Burke, *Public Order*, 22-23.

Some might view this as a philosophy already in vogue. Without the sanction of law, however, it detracts from the international order by appealing to preponderant force for protection instead of the authority of a law that might be beneficial to all states. Codifying parameters of unneutral non-belligerent conduct could turn this situation around.

While this seems more paradox than panacea, it is an alternative that accommodates restraint. Expediency benefitting all is not anathema to international law; it is the foundation of many customary rules. Trying to change the law through practice alone though will ensure the law will be written in blood—but let it not be the blood of the American Bluejacket.

General Prescriptions for Naval Policy

It is worth restating that policy must be developed in general terms to control actions in specific cases. The parameters that policy must observe are defined by these general rules:

- Remember any rights you assert are also obligations to submit to similar rights of all others
- When force is appropriate use only as much as the situation requires
- Do not let political labels be confused with legal reality.[14]

Unneutral behavior leaves the naval force in a situation where the options for forceful actions are only of a defensive character, therefore, regardless of their state of readiness, at the moment they are first engaged there is great potential to accept a tactical disadvantage. Accurate and timely warning of risk becomes paramount.

The instructions to the at-sea commander must be candid and specific, imposing all necessary legal restraint while offering every appropriate tactical latitude. This is a difficult mix to say the least.

The advantages held by potential adversaries may not argue for restraint on their part. In the current context, the decision when to stop accepting less than impartial behavior belongs to

---

[14]Rubin, "Rules of Thumb for Gut Decisions: International Law in Emergencies," 44-47.

the aggrieved belligerent. The at-sea commander must be given every opportunity to anticipate when that decision will be made.

These situations require well-planned and clearly stated Operations Orders, well-armed and highly alert forces, an understanding of the legal situation, and an understanding by all concerned of both the importance of restraint and the lethality of hesitating to respond at the instant self-defense becomes appropriate. "A strategist should think in terms of paralyzing, not killing . . . psychological pressure on the government of a country may suffice to cancel all the resources at its command."[15] Where that effect is not anticipated, our forces need to proceed fully alerted with a complete understanding of the law and the rights they are defending.

CONCLUSION

Policymakers will continue to call upon the peacetime (and hopefully peaceful) employment of naval forces for a variety of national, coalition, and multi-national operations. This only can be considered an effective option, however, if the officers charged with executing the naval policy of the United States continue to have the necessary resources: adequate forces, domestic and international political consensus, and a clear understanding of the U.S. and competing views of the legal situation.

Operations should be planned and executed with these issues of law in mind:

• Will these operations change the status, or the perceived status, of the United States under the laws of war and neutrality?

• Are "rights" or "interests" being cited as the motivation for these operations?

• Is the potential adversary in these operations likely to perceive he needs to use force in self-defense or in defense of "rights" asserted?

• Will these operations establish precedents that are to the long-term advantage or disadvantage of the United States?

• Will these operations potentially add belligerent parties

---

[15]Liddell Hart, 228.

to an existing armed conflict?

• Do the naval forces at sea have sufficient information about the law asserted by the United States and and that asserted by any potential adversaries to execute these operations in a manner which advances U.S. policy?

The truly competent naval officer has respect for both physical and legal environments, based on the realization that either can unleash forces that can destroy his ship. Change for the worse in the physical environment can turn loose powers of nature that can destroy anything man has made. Changes in the legal environment can, in turn, bring on dangerous changes in the tactical environment and bring the destructive powers of man to bear. It is perhaps his respect for these forces that allows the naval officer to go to sea confident of his ability to meet its challenges. The naval officer in command at sea owes respect for the physical environment to his crew and his ship if he is to keep them safe; he owes respect for the legal environment to his nation if he is to deserve the special trust and confidence placed in him to support and execute policy without unnecessary losses to his unit or the prestige of the nation.

Count Wachtmeister noted that for Sweden, "Foreign policy is the first line of defense."[16] A thoughtfully developed and well-coordinated naval policy certainly enhances the defense of the United States. These recommendations were made in the hope they might help in crafting our naval policy.

---

[16]Wachtmeister lecture.

THE AUTHOR

Captain John N. Petrie, USN, is professor of National Security Policy and Director of Research at the National War College. He has spent his career in destroyers and is en route to duty as Commander, Destroyer Squadron 32. Ashore his assignments have included duty on the Joint Staff and special assignments with State Department and National Security Council teams. Captain Petrie is a Distinguished Graduate of the Naval War College, where he served as a Research Associate and completed Senior Service College at the National War College, where he was a Senior Research Fellow. He holds an AB from Villanova University and the MALD and Ph.D. degrees from the Fletcher School of Law and Diplomacy. Besides being the editor of *Essays on Strategy XI* and *Essays on Strategy XII* (NDU Press), Captain Petrie has had his writings published by the U.S. Naval Institute, *Naval War College Review, Joint Force Quarterly (JFQ)*, the United Nations Association—National Capital Area, and the *Fletcher Forum.*

McNair Papers

The McNair Papers are published at Fort Lesley J. McNair, home of the Institute for National Strategic Studies and the National Defense University. An Army post since 1794, the fort was given its present name in 1948 in honor of Lieutenant General Lesley James McNair. General McNair, known as "Educator of the Army" and trainer of some three million troops, was about to take command of Allied ground forces in Europe under Eisenhower, when he was killed in combat in Normandy, 25 July 1944.

The following is a complete listing of published McNair Papers. For information on the availability of specific titles, contact the Circulation Manager, Publications Directorate & NDU Press, Fort Lesley J. McNair, Washington, DC 30219-6000 (telephone: commercial 202/475-1913; DSN 335-1913).

1. Joseph P. Lorenz, *Egypt and the New Arab Coalition*, February 1989.
2. John E. Endicott, *Grand Strategy and the Pacific Region*, May 1989.
3. Eugene V. Rostow, *President, Prime Minister, or Constitutional Monarch?*, October 1989.
4. Howard G. DeWolf, *SDI and Arms Control*, November 1989.
5. Martin C. Libicki, *What Makes Industries Strategic*, November 1989.
6. Melvin A. Goodman, *Gorbachev and Soviet Policy in the Third World*, February 1990.
7. John Van Oudenaren, "The Tradition of Change in Soviet Foreign Policy," and Francis Conte, "Two Schools of Soviet Diplomacy," in *Understanding Soviet Foreign Policy*, April 1990.
8. Max G. Manwaring and Court Prisk, *A Strategic View of Insurgencies: Insights from El Salvador*, May 1990.
9. Steven R. Linke, *Managing Crises in Defense Industry: The PEPCON and Avtex Cases*, June 1990.
10. Christine M. Helms, *Arabism and Islam: Stateless Nations and Nationless States*, September 1990.
11. Ralph A. Cossa, *Iran: Soviet Interests, US Concerns*, July 1990.
12. Ewan Jamieson, *Friend or Ally? A Question for New Zealand*, May 1991.
13. Richard J. Dunn III, *From Gettysburg to the Gulf and Beyond: Coping with Revolutionary Technological Change in Land Warfare*, March 1992.
14. Ted Greenwood, *U.S. and NATO Force Structure and Military Operations in the Mediterranean*, June 1993.

15. Oscar W. Clyatt, Jr., *Bulgaria's Quest for Security After the Cold War*, February 1993.

16. William C. Bodie, *Moscow's "Near Abroad": Security Policy in Post-Soviet Europe*, June 1993.

17. William H. Lewis (ed.), *Military Implications of United Nations Peacekeeping Operations*, June 1993.

18. Sterling D. Sessions and Carl R. Jones, *Interoperability: A Desert Storm Case Study*, July 1993.

19. Eugene V. Rostow, *Should Article 43 of the United Nations Charter Be Raised From the Dead?* July 1993

20. William T. Johnsen and Thomas Durell-Young; Jeffrey Simon; Daniel N. Nelson; William C. Bodie, and James McCarthy, *European Security Toward the Year 2000*, August 1993.

21. Edwin R. Carlisle, ed., *Developing Battlefield Technologies in the 1990s*, August 1993.

22. Patrick Clawson, *How Has Saddam Hussein Survived? Economic Sanctions, 1990–93*, August 1993.

23. Jeffrey Simon, *Czechoslovakia's "Velvet Divorce," Visegrad Cohesion, and European Fault Lines*, October 1993.

24. Eugene V. Rostow, *The Future of Palestine*, November 1993.

25. William H. Lewis, John Mackinlay, John G. Ruggie, and Sir Brian Urquhart, *Peacekeeping: The Way Ahead?* November 1993.

26. Edward Marks and William Lewis, *Triage for Failing States*, January 1994.

27. Gregory D. Foster, *In Search of a Post-Cold War Security Structure*, February 1994.

28. Martin C. Libicki, *The Mesh and the Net: Speculations on Armed Conflict in a Time of Free Silicon*, March 1994.

29. Patrick Clawson, ed., *Iran's Strategic Intentions and Capabilities*, April 1994.

30. James W. Morrison, *Vladimir Zhirinovskiy: An Assessment of a Russian Ultra-Nationalist*, April 1994.

31. Patrick M. Cronin and Michael J. Green, *Redefining the U.S.-Japan Alliance: Tokyo's National Defense Program*, November 1994.

32. Scott W. Conrad, *Moving the Force:* Desert Storm *and Beyond*, December 1994.

33. John N. Petrie, *American Neutrality in the 20th Century: The Impossible Dream*, January 1995

34. James H. Brusstar and Ellen Jones, *The Russian Military's Role in Politics*, January 1995.

www.ingramcontent.com/pod-product-compliance
Lightning Source LLC
Chambersburg PA
CBHW070013300526
45794CB00001B/305